Instagram Marketing

How to Dominate Your Niche in 2019 with Your Small Business and Personal Brand by Marketing on a Super Popular Social Media Platform and Leveraging its Influencers

Contents

Introduction

Instagram is one of the hottest social media platforms in the world right now and for a good reason. It offers many unique opportunities for businesses to grow their audience, get in front of prospects, and start making sales through the internet. If you are running a business, or if you are planning on starting one, using Instagram to your advantage is necessary if you desire to create maximum growth in your business in 2019. Whether you like it or not, Instagram is here to stay, and your audience loves spending time on it, no matter who your audience may be.

As Instagram continues to grow, the opportunities to connect with your audience and provide valuable content and information grows as well. Instagram has always been a visual storytelling social media platform as it started out having feeds filled with beautiful photographs and people sharing their stories through images. Over the past two years, Instagram has expanded to include stories, live videos, and now IGTV which can all be incorporated into your branding and outreach strategies. As you will learn about in this book, the more ways that you generate interaction with your audience through Instagram, the more followers you will gain and the greater traction you will have on this platform.

If you desire to create success in your own business, you need to take advantage of as many of these ways as possible and learn how to work them together to generate success with your brand on Instagram. In this book, *Instagram Marketing: How to Dominate Your Niche in 2019 with Your Small Business and Personal Brand by Marketing on a Super Popular Social Media Platform and Leveraging Its Influencers,* you are going to discover exactly what you need to do to generate success in your business on Instagram in 2019. Whether you are just launching your business or if you are starting a brand new one, everything that you need to know, including all of the strategies and tips that you can put into action right away, are shared within this book.

This book is all-inclusive of all of the best strategies, so it may seem like a lot to dive into, especially if you are brand new to the platform. For that reason, you may want to take your time, read it in order, and ease yourself into the process of building on Instagram to reach your target audience. The more you take your time and master each step, the easier it will be for you to generate and maintain your own Instagram strategy so that you can create continued success on the platform. As you will learn about in this book, success is not guaranteed on any platform, but you can maximize your chances and grow to your largest potential by employing the strategies shared inside this book.

If you are ready to launch on Instagram or start growing your following massively and take advantage of the new marketing trends in 2019, it is time to get started! Remember: take your time and implement everything intentionally and to the best of your ability. The more you implement new practices, the easier it will become, and the larger your following will grow over time. As with anything, Instagram has a learning curve, but hopefully, this book will help you move through that learning curve as quickly as possible so that you can start experiencing success right away.

Chapter 1: Instagram's Popularity

It is not a secret that Instagram is one of the most popular social media platforms out there next to Facebook, YouTube, and Twitter.

Since being purchased by Facebook back in 2013, Instagram has evolved drastically and has become one of the best social media networking platforms for small businesses and personal brands who are looking to get in front of their audience and have a major impact. If you have not already gotten on Instagram, you are going to need to make Instagram a priority in 2019, as it will be one of the best ways for you to expand your business to get in front of a larger portion of your audience. If you are already building your brand on Instagram, 2019 will be another great year for massive expansion.

Why Instagram is so Popular

One of the biggest benefits of Instagram is that it combines the positive features of all other social networking sites in a way that no other platform does. Instagram has the live video features like Facebook, the IGTV channel features like YouTube, photo sharing options, story sharing options like Snapchat, a great discovery page like Twitter, and private messenger like most other platforms. When you are on Instagram, you have many unique ways to share information with your audience so that they can get a fully engaged brand experience, which allows them to begin creating many associations and connections with you and your company.

Instagram's most unique feature is the photo-based sharing newsfeeds which allow those who are visually inclined to *see* the stories or interesting features that are attractive to them, rather than have to read about it. Since most people are on social media platforms to scroll and consume information quickly, being able to see and gather plenty of information in ten seconds or less makes Instagram highly popular. While certain posts will capture an individual's attention longer or draw their interest into the caption, many times, it is just the overall visual appeal that draws people in and has them wanting to engage with the brand and learn more about who the company is.

Although Instagram is highly popular, one of the best features is that there are not quite as many users as Facebook. Facebook has virtually every demographic on it, whereas Instagram has a more unique demographic which ranges from 18-45 years old, which means that, for most brands who are trying to target the younger or middle-aged generations, Instagram is a clearer space to be on. In most cases, it is actually easier to be located on Instagram than it is to be located on Facebook. However, even if your target audience is on both and you want to utilize both platforms to your advantage, the fact that Facebook owns Instagram offers many unique inter-platform sharing features such as managing advertisements from one account while running them on both platforms. With that in mind, Instagram has a lot to offer that many other social sharing sites just do not.

Why You Need to Use Instagram

In 2019, most individuals who are shopping through new companies are also going to be looking to follow them online and engage with them in the online space. If your brand is primarily run online, being plugged into social networking sites is your best opportunity to create more dynamic relationships with your audience so that they can connect with you through your online platform. In 2019, if you are not on Instagram, chances are your audience is not going to be able to find you online at all and start building important relationships with you, so instead, they will likely choose to follow someone else. In other words, if you are not actively getting in front of your audience and building relationships, someone else is going to do it, and they will have a better time targeting and creating connections with your audience. If you are not actively taking action towards making this happen for your business, you will quickly be forgotten about.

In the modern world, people rely heavily on social proof to determine whether or not a company is worth buying into, especially if that company is primarily online or if they are going to be engaging with that company online because they do not live near a physical location. These days, social proof is built by having a brand that is already established online, which has a large audience and a strong engagement from that audience. The more you are interacting with your audience and having them sing your praises after working with you or buying your products, the more other people who locate your business are going to come to trust you and believe in your offerings. Naturally, this increased interest and the proof that you are trustworthy will increase your ability to make sales through your online platform, or bring more people into your storefront to make sales there.

Finally, getting on Instagram proves to your audience that you are modern and that you are "staying with the times". Most audiences want to see that the people they are working with are up-to-date on using the latest platforms and interactive features, as this proves that they are still relevant. In this modern world, where brand names matter and whom you know is paramount, proving that you are someone worth knowing and who people can be proud about doing business with is important. You need to make sure that your audience knows that you are worth their time, and then you need to make sure that you use their time wisely so that they can gain value from every single thing they see through you. As you will learn about later in this book, that value can be anything from providing entertainment so that you can build relationships to providing new relevant products so that you can gain sales.

Who is Already on Instagram

Essentially everyone who is worth knowing in your industry already exists on Instagram, which is one of the biggest reasons why you need to be on Instagram as well. Any major brand that has a large following is already on Instagram, and everyone who would be interested in following these brands is on Instagram as well. The Instagram world typically consists of three sectors of people: those who are running businesses and use Instagram to sell, influencers who are helping those businesses market their products, and customers who are paying attention to the latest trends in their preferred markets. If you want to start making more sales, leveraging social media, and maximizing your profits through the internet, getting on Instagram and investing some time in understanding how to grow your account and build it into a sales funnel is necessary. By effectively fitting Instagram into your overall marketing strategy, and having a proper Instagram strategy for marketing to your audience, you can ensure that you are making a wider reach and broadening your audience in a meaningful way.

Chapter 2: How Instagram Can Benefit You

Instagram has many things to offer, beyond the wide range of features that are available so that you can provide the most interactive brand experience possible. Naturally, you want to make sure that everywhere you invest time into your business is actually going to pay off so that you are not wasting your time on strategies that will fail to provide you with results in the end. Fortunately, Instagram has many valuable benefits that make this platform worthy of any business' attention, since virtually every business model can find a way to work Instagram into their strategy and maximize their brand awareness, and therefore, sales.

Instagram Statistics

On Instagram, 71% of 18-24-year-old individuals are using the platform to connect with friends, family members, influencers, and brands that they enjoy following. Of this sector, more than 35% of these individuals check the platform multiple times daily, and another 22% check it at least once per day. This means that, if you position yourself correctly, you can reach up to 57% or more of your target audience through just one properly created, positioned, and scheduled post.

It's not just those who are 18-24 years old who spend time on Instagram. In fact, 30% of the users are aged between 25 and 34 years old, and another 17% are aged between 35-44 years old. There are more than one billion active monthly users on Instagram, which means that there is a massive opportunity to connect with the right people and start making serious waves in your business.

Aside from the statistics of which demographics are spending the most time on Instagram, it is also worth noting that all of these individuals are interested in a wide range of niches. That means that they are willing to follow almost any brand that interests them, regardless of what niche that brand is from. There are even dentists who are making a massive impact on Instagram, which is huge considering that many people are afraid of the dentist! By connecting with their audiences through this platform, businesses of all shapes and sizes can start creating positive connections with their audience, which means that they can increase their brand recognition and their revenue simply by being on Instagram.

Who Will Benefit from Instagram

Brands and small businesses of all shapes and sizes can benefit from getting on Instagram, though those who are targeting audiences in the 18-44-year-old range are going to have the best opportunity to connect with their target audience. The reality is that, as long as your target audience falls in this range, you need to be on Instagram because your audience *will* look for you, and if they cannot find you, they will look for someone else who offers what you offer. Even if you are just using a light marketing strategy with minimal time spent on Instagram, at least creating a memorable and consistent image on the platform will support you in getting located and creating those relationships that will prove to be invaluable in the future.

How People are Using Instagram

Some business owners or brands may be having a hard time envisioning how a picture-based sharing platform could be used to benefit their brands. While we are going to go into deeper explanations and strategies later on in this book, we want you to gain some inspiration around how your unique niche can be leveraged on Instagram so that you can begin to create an image in your mind around how Instagram will benefit your business. Here is a list of several different business models and how they are uniquely using the Instagram platform to connect with their target audience:

- Makeup artists are using the platform to share new makeup looks, products, and techniques for people to try.
- Dentists are using the platform to create a positive, friendly visual image of their office so that their audience can begin associating the dentist with a happy, stress-free place.
- Lawyers are using the platform to connect with people who may need their support and are formulating visual images of authority and concern to prove that they care.
- Clothing companies are using Instagram to show off new styles with the clothes they offer, to inspire people to create their own unique looks and showcase new products.
- Business coaches and life coaches are using Instagram to create a visual image of what someone's life or business could be like, and then positioning themselves as the experts to teach those individuals how to create that lifestyle for themselves.
- Daycares are showing off their activities, their learning opportunities, and their staff so that potential new families can see how positive and interactive the daycare is.
- Dance studios are sharing images and videos of their dancers, their competitions, and their highlight moments to showcase their talents and inspire new students to join their studios.

- Restaurants are showcasing their most delectable dishes, families enjoying time spent in the restaurant, and the individuals making and serving the food to create a welcoming image for their target audience.
- Influencers are using Instagram to position themselves as experts in their niche so that people can turn to them to gain information about new products and services that they should be trying out. These are like the professional reviewers on the internet these days!
- Network marketers are using Instagram to show how their unique products can fit into a daily lifestyle so that people are inspired to begin working with them or purchasing their products.

Countless other niches are using Instagram to generate an image for their brand and attract people into their audience so that they can market to more people. Through using the image feed and stories, brands can create a very specific image for their audience that allows them to visually associate brands with their ideal "look" or feel. For example, if you want to create family-friendly, wholesome, clean, positive images, you can do so by curating a newsfeed and story feed that reflect these things in everything that you share. The more people that land on your page or watch your stories, the more consistently they will become exposed to these feelings and images, and therefore, the more consistently they will begin associating you with being the person that they are looking for to fulfill their needs.

If you did not see your niche listed, rest assured that there is definitely a way for you uniquely to put together the videos, stories, and photograph features so that you can begin interacting with your audience as well. Throughout the rest of this book, you will learn about unique ways that you can create an image for your brand and leverage these features to serve your business model.

Chapter 3: The 2019 Instagram Evolution

As Instagram is now going into its ninth year in business, it has definitely evolved throughout the years as new features are continually made available, and people begin incorporating those new features into their user experiences. In 2019, it is expected that the evolution will continue as we learn how to use these features in new ways to offer unique brand experiences for our audiences. Naturally, you do not want to enter 2019 using outdated strategies to attempt to target your audience, so before we begin looking into specific strategies and approaches, we are going to dig into some 2019 specific marketing trends and strategies that you will need to look out for.

Of course, it is challenging to predict exactly what will come in the new year. We cannot guarantee as to what new features may become available and how updates to the app may change the way that we use it when it comes to interacting with your audience. However, it is pretty clear that certain trends are already growing in popularity, and it is not incredibly challenging to keep track of upcoming trends as long as you learn how to stay engaged.

Trends to Look Out For in 2019

Instagram, like any platform, is filled with trends that you can easily identify as long as you are paying attention and engaging with the app on a regular basis. While trends can be hard to predict, there are five trends that we suspect will rise on the Instagram platform in 2019.

The first trend, IGTV, launched in June of 2018, but we expect to see it take off and grow even larger in 2019. This platform is dedicated to those who use Instagram on their mobile devices and give individuals the opportunity to follow YouTube-like channels through the Instagram platform. Unlike other video services, however, IGTV is dedicated to vertical video formatting which makes it perfect for use on mobile devices, as it offers the ability to see the most video over your screen. Individuals who are seeking to expand into their mobile audience and start creating more content for their followers to pay attention to can leverage IGTV for a variety of different uses, from sharing pieces of wisdom or knowledge in your niche to sharing how-to videos and tutorials. There are many ways that IGTV can be used to generate sales, but the best way is to ultimately get in front of your audience and start talking about your brand and the ways that you can support your audience through either your products or services. The key here, however, is to refrain

14

from making it all sound too salesy. Instead of talking for five minutes about your service, for example, spend that time building knowledge and offering tips that relate to your audience's problems or pain points and then propose your product or service as a solution. This way, your audience has a valid reason to stay around and listen, rather than it feeling like you have simply provided them with a prolonged advertisement for them to watch.

2) The second trend to rise in 2019 will be the rise of micro-brands, or small businesses, who are sharing and getting connected with their audiences. In the past, Instagram has continued to evolve to shine spotlights on small business owners, entrepreneurs, and local brands. It is believed that in 2019, this trend will continue to rise and will make it even easier for micro-brands to connect with their audiences and create an extra income stream through Instagram marketing. The biggest reason why this is likely expanding in trends is because Instagram offers many different ways to share your brand with your audience intimately, and people like sharing that personal connection with the brands they support. Most larger brands simply do not have the time or the means to offer that intimate relationship with their audience, which is why people are increasingly leaning toward following micro-brands. As a small business owner or a personal brand yourself, having the spotlight being shined primarily on brands just like yours means now is the perfect time to get on Instagram and start building relationships with customers who are looking for exactly what you offer!

3) The third trend to rise on Instagram in 2019 will be using story advertisements. If you are already on Instagram, you may see sponsored ads rising between the stories that you are watching. These paid advertisements are an opportunity to share screen time with your audience so that they can find your brand and begin following you in the online space. However, you do not have to use paid advertisements to get your advertising on in the story feature! The number of templates for story layouts is increasing, meaning that you can use the story feature to generate advertisements and

simply share them to your regular story. While these will not go as far and can only be seen by your existing audience or those who locate you and choose to watch your stories, they can still be a great opportunity to leverage your stories for advertisement purposes.

(4) The fourth trend coming up is e-commerce shops, or the opportunity to begin integrating e-commerce-related features into your page which makes it easier for customers to locate you and to actually shop through you. The most noteworthy feature that offers this right now would be shoppable posts, which allow you to post static images with products in them and then tag the products so that customers can be taken directly to a checkout link. That way, you can post something and encourage people to shop with you through your product tags on your posts. A great example of people doing this would be those who sell clothing or accessories sharing images featuring their products and then saying "shop the look!" so that people pause and look at the image. If they like it, they can easily tap the tags on the post and start shopping for the products that they desire. These posts do require a Facebook page integration feature to work, but once you set it up, this feature is incredible and it is expected that it will evolve to be even more interactive in the coming months.

(5) The fifth trend is one that happens every year in social media and is expected to continue this year. That is – Instagram will be looking for ways to increase engagement with their audience so that their audience spends more time on Instagram. For Instagram, the more popular their platform is, the more people are going to be likely to use it to build their brands and sell their products, which means that Instagram stands to have more paid advertisements going through its platform. This means that they want to drive as much traffic to the platform as possible, make it even more enjoyable for everyone on the platform, and keep brands and customers connecting on the platform so that they can continue making money. In other words – Instagram wins when they help small businesses win too, which

means that Instagram will continue creating features to help out brands just like yours so that they can continue to grow too.

Chapter 4: Creating a Branded Account

Navigating the Instagram platform requires you to set up an account and begin building that account first. In this chapter, we are going to explore how you can set up an Instagram account and begin navigating the platform as a brand so that you can get started reaping in the benefits of Instagram in 2019. If you already have an account, you should still pay attention to this chapter as you will gain plenty of important information on how to navigate your business account and set it up so that you can run a powerful and memorable brand.

Getting Started on Instagram

Creating your Instagram account is best done on a mobile device, as Instagram has been optimized for mobile usage. While you can still create your account on the desktop version of the platform, it may not be as easy as it can be and sometimes be more challenging to navigate and there are fewer features available on the desktop version of Instagram. So to get started, you will want to go into the application feature on your cell phone and download Instagram from your app store. Once the app has been downloaded, you can launch it and follow the on-screen process for creating your account, which will include inputting either your email or phone number and then choosing a password. Once you have done that, the next page will require you to choose a username for your account.

Choosing Your Handle

The Instagram handle that you choose needs to be clear and easy to remember; otherwise, your audience may not be able to find you again once they leave your account. As well, you want to make sure that the moment people see your username, they can make some form of clear connection between who you are and what your company does; otherwise, they may not be tempted to click onto your profile page.

In general, most brands will simply use their company names for their handles, as this makes it easy for you to be found on Instagram. For example, Nike, Adidas, Walmart, and Nordstrom all use their brand names for their usernames on social media platforms, as this makes it straightforward for them to be located. If you are a personal brand, you may need to change the way you approach your social media to ensure that you can be located and recognized by those around the internet. Generally, personal brands will continue to follow the same rule of thumb as other brands will by using their names as their usernames. For example, Kendall Jenner's username is simply @kendalljenner, making it easier for her to be discovered online. There are, however, some exceptions to this rule of thumb when you are creating a personal brand online. For example, if you are someone who has a long, challenging name or one that has complex spelling, using it for your username will likely result in you not being located online. In this case, you can use a nickname for your username and then use that same nickname everywhere online, or you can use an easier spelling of your name. For example, Nicki Minaj's real name is Onika Tanya Maraj, but this would be difficult to remember and spell; therefore, she personally branded herself as Nicki Minaj. This makes it easier for her fans to locate her online, and anywhere else where they may seek her out, which makes her personal brand both memorable and simple to locate.

When you are making your username, refrain from using odd spelling, usernames that are similar to what has already been used online, or different characters or numbers in your username. Unless your character or number is a part of your brand name, attempting to make your username unique by adding these characters will instead just make it more challenging for you to be located. Remember, this is how people are going to look you up, and this is the name that people are going to remember you by. If you want to have people easily able to recall you and locate you, you need to create both a username and a brand that people will remember.

After you have created your username, you will be taken to the main screen where you can begin navigating the application. Here, you continue to fill out a few more parts of your profile before you begin interacting with anyone on the platform. You do not want to be putting in work to connect with your target audience if your profile is still not developed enough for people to identify you to ensure that no connection is a missed connection.

Crafting the Perfect Bio

Once you have created your username, the next piece of copy that you are going to need to write is your bio. On Instagram, your bio can be up to 150 characters in length and can include links to other profiles and hashtags that may be relevant to your brand. Your bio gives you the opportunity to let people know who you are and what you are about, though you can also use it to leverage sales and market your business through your profile. Using your bio wisely is the best way to ensure that you can use it to increase your memorability, as well as the amount of interaction that people will have in following you and supporting your brand.

When it comes to writing a bio that will actually help you make sales, there are three things that you need to focus on: catchiness, informative, and promotional. You want your bio to be catchy enough that people are interested in actually reading it, informative so that people can get a feel for who you are and what your company is about, and promotional so that people are more likely to click on the link that you can provide for them.

look at other bios (property) idea

Typically, complete sentences are frowned upon in bios unless you are using a single short sentence, so refrain from using anything too excessive or wordy. In most bios, rather than using sentences, people simply share lists of their interests or what their brand is all about. Writing your bio properly is essential, so be sure to take the time to identify what is actually going to work for you and your brand. The best way to get a good feel for what will work for your unique brand is to go to the pages of other brands in your niche and read through their bios so that you can see what works and what does not. Take a look at the bios of those who are succeeding versus the bios of those who have not yet accumulated a large following and see if you can notice any trends or differences that seem to set the two apart. You want to be emulating successful brands, of course, so attempt to recreate trends that they are using in their bios through your own bio, but more authentically so that it resonates with your brand and your unique target audience.

In addition to writing your bio, you are also going to want to share the link to your website so that people can see more about who you are and have the opportunity to shop online if you have an online storefront. If you have many links that you would like to share with people, consider using a service like Link Tree, which allows you to create a professional, personally branded landing page that has buttons to the various websites you want to direct your audience to. If you are marketing multiple things on your account, such as a freebie offer, your signature offer, and the opportunity to follow you elsewhere online, these different links can make it easier for you to direct your audience around to your services or other accounts. Regardless of how you choose to structure your link, make sure that you do provide one so that people can click to it and get a deeper feel for who you are and what you have to offer.

The following are great bios that can be used for your brand. Of course, you will need to adapt your bio to suit your unique brand or niche, but these will give you a great starting point to get a feel for what works and what sells when it comes to bios:

- A gourmet cheese company: "Gourmet Cheese. The Right Wine. A Great Party. Need We Say More? #linkinthebio"
- A fashion blogger: "23 // Fashion // NYC // Lattes and Lipstick. Shop my outfits at the link below!"
- A life coach: "Chasing goals, living big, enjoying life. Live your best life – check out the link below!"
- A jewelry company: "Diamonds for every occasion. #Linkinthebio"
- A local limo company: "Ride in style for less – Vancouver/Calgary/Toronto. Book at the link below."

Uploading Your Profile Picture

Your profile is going to require a picture as well, which will provide your audience with the opportunity to visually see who you are and begin to make the connection between your name and your image. When it comes to making branded accounts, you have two options with your profile picture: upload an image of your logo, or upload an image of yourself. Which you choose will depend on what type of company you are running and which image you want people to remember.

For most companies, the logo will suffice as this is the easiest way to begin building brand recognition through your business. As people come to associate your logo and username with each other, they will also come to recognize your logo and identify it anywhere else where they may spot it. This can be huge for brand recognition, which is why if you are running a company, your logo is the only thing that your profile picture should be. Make sure that you upload a high-resolution image and that it fits perfectly in the profile image circle so that your logo can be seen. If it is blurry or hard to understand, people may simply skip over it because they are unsure as to what it is that they are looking at.

If you are branding yourself, you may prefer to use an image of your face rather than an image of your logo as personal brands typically seek to inspire brand recognition through facial recognition. Make sure that you use a clear photo that accurately reflects your brand so that it makes sense with the overall image that you are attempting to create. For example, if you are a travel blogger, use an image of you with a great outdoor backdrop that will help people make the connection. If you are a real estate agent, have an image of you smiling in front of a home or a blank wall so that you have the emphasis on yourself and your influence as a salesperson. Do not use selfies, poor quality images, or images that seem out of place in this space as this can result in people feeling confused around your brand, which can lead to fewer followers, and therefore, fewer sales.

You should be leveraging every single aspect of your page to create one uniform image that accurately reflects your brand image.

Make sure that you never leave your profile image empty, as people will not trust or interact with companies that have not yet uploaded profile images. Refrain from interacting with anyone until this has been done, as most people who see profiles without images will assume that these profiles are either scammers or not yet interesting enough to pay attention to. The profiles with attractive, clean, high-quality profile images that look enticing are the ones that end up getting followers, so wait until you have filled this in before engaging with people's content or following anyone.

Important Instagram Settings

Instagram is optimal for businesses, which is why so many micro-brands are using it to

connect with their audiences. On Instagram, there are a variety of important settings that you should adjust to ensure that your profile is ready to support a growing brand, because this way, you can get the most out of the platform. There are four things that you need to do when you launch a branded account that should be done right away: switching to a business account (so that you can run paid advertisements,) adjusting your privacy settings, turning on two-factor authentication, and adjusting story shares.

Switching to a Business Account

Switching your account to a business account is simple. You do so by going into the settings for your account, which can be located at the three lines in the top right corner of the homepage. From there, go to the "Account" option and tap "Switch to Business Account". If you do not already have one, Instagram will help you quickly set up a Facebook page which your Instagram business account will be linked to. This step is necessary, even if you do not plan on using a Facebook page, as it allows you to engage in certain exclusive business activities on Instagram, such as tagging products in your photographs, running paid promotions, and setting an address or location for your business on Instagram if you have one.

Once you have switched to having a business account, Instagram will also give you access to important analytical information. This information will ensure that you can track your success through monitoring the success of posts, monitoring your follower growth, and even get a clear outline as to who your demographic is and whether or not you are effectively reaching the right people through the platform. This makes the business features on Instagram even more valuable. While a business account is not necessary for running a business on Instagram, if you desire to get any traction and really build your business account on Instagram, you will want to have access to all of the business exclusive features that they offer.

Adjusting Privacy Settings

On Instagram, certain privacy settings can be used to limit who can see your account and what can be seen or done on your account. You are going to want to go in and make sure that any privacy settings which may be turned "on" are turned "off" to ensure that your privacy settings are hiding no part of your account. Make sure that people can comment on and share your posts, follow you, and message you back through your stories so that people can engage with your profile in as many different ways as possible. Keeping your account private in any way can lead to people not being able to engage with you, which can reduce people's desire to follow you because one of the main reasons why people are on social media is to build relationships with others. You need to be available for the relationship building process!

Two-Factor Authentication

Two-factor authentication is necessary for anyone who wants to run a business online as it ensures that people cannot hack your account and block you out of it. Two-factor authentication will require you to approve of all new logins either through your phone number or email address, which means that if anyone attempts to log into your account remotely so that they can hack you, they will not be able to get in without your code. You can enable two-factor authentication by going back into your settings menu, tapping "Privacy and Security" and then tapping "Two-factor authentication". There, you will be walked through the process of verifying either your phone number or an email address that can be used to make your account more secure.

If you do ever receive a request to log in and you have not attempted to log in on a new browser, it is important that you immediately change your password on Instagram. If you have received the code, this is proof that someone has identified what your password is and has successfully logged into your account. Of course, they will be stuck in the login process since they do not have your verification code to complete the two-factor authentication login, but this still means that your account has been compromised. By changing your password, you can ensure that no one can somehow hack into your account and begin compromising your business through Instagram.

Chapter 5: Five Unwritten Rules of Instagram

Getting on Instagram and going big right off the bat means knowing how to play "large" on Instagram like an experienced pro, even if you do not yet have the experience of someone who has been on the platform for a long time. Over time, you will discover tricks and techniques of your own, but to help you get started, here is a list of five unwritten rules of Instagram to help you start out strong. If you begin by using these strategies from day one, you can feel confident that your Instagram will grow rapidly and effectively.

Post at the Right Time

On Instagram, your audience will tend to hang out on the platform at different times throughout the day and week. Learning how to track your best posting times and post within these peak hours will ensure that your photographs get maximum engagement so that you can begin growing your account rapidly. With Instagram, the algorithm favors posts that are being interacted with quickly and genuinely, so the more likes and comments that you can accumulate early on, the better.

You can track the right posting times for yourself and your audience through Instagram's business analytics or through third-party applications like PLANN or Iconosquare, which both have intelligent and highly accurate schedules for you to plan your posts with. These platforms track your engagement and let you know when your profile tends to get the most views, likes, and comments through your new posts. Although third-party apps will cost money to gain access to this information, it can help you rapidly grow your platform through having access to the right information to help you do so.

In addition to using the right posting times, make sure that you are using the right hashtag sequences which will ensure that you actually have the opportunity to get seen. While you will learn more about hashtags later, it is important that you understand right away that your hashtags are your key opportunity for getting seen on Instagram. To put it simply: images without hashtags will have no access to new, untapped audience members which means that anytime you post without using hashtags, you are leaving money on the table with your Instagram account.

Exercise Selfie Control

The trend on Instagram used to be to load your page up with selfies and have people liking your images, and while this behavior is still perfectly okay for simple sharing accounts, they are not ideal for brands or businesses who are looking to grow their platform in 2019. While selfies can (and should) be used to grow your page, you should refrain from having every post, or even every other post featuring you in a selfie. Instead, use selfies sparingly and place emphasis on uploading other photos of interest to help you increase your reach in 2019.

If you do love to share selfies and they do in some way relate to your brand, consider using your selfies more consistently in your story feed and less frequently in your actual newsfeed. This way, you can still share on-brand selfie images that can help you increase traction, but they do not dominate your feed and make you appear unprofessional or juvenile on the platform. These days, people prefer to see more thoughtful images that look similar to those that would be taken by professional photographers. Even if you do not have a professional photographer readily available to photograph you, consider getting someone else to snap your photos, or using a tripod and a selfie timer to get better quality images that do not feature an elongated view of your right bicep.

Despite selfies not being ideal, people do still like to see other humans in the images that they are looking at, as this creates a more personal touch in your photographs. So, while you want to refrain from overdoing it on the selfies, you do want to ensure that there are still humans in your photographs so that your profile can attract more attention from your target audience.

Be Original

The longer social media dominates the online space the more people are looking for authentic connections with original brands and companies. Simply put: people do not want to feel like they are following an overly strategized advertisement account that lacks personality or originality. Your target audience is following you on Instagram because they want to feel *connected* to you, not because they want to be advertised to 24/7. If you are going to make a strong connection with your audience, you need to find a way to be original, create a unique image for your company, and stand out from the rest of the people who are targeting your audience.

If you are running a professional company, such as a law firm or a dentist office, finding a way to be original may be challenging as you want to ensure that you are authentically engaging without taking away from your professional expert appeal. Still, there are ways that you can generate an authentic image without tarnishing your professionalism or scaring away your audience for fear of them following you solely to be advertised to. A great way to find out unique ways to share your originality in your niche industry is to look up your competitors online and see what they are doing. Typically, the ones who are dominating the space have a very unique and original approach, and you can learn a thing or two from these individuals.

Of course, once you are done with your search, you need to find ways that you can incorporate the tips, ideas, and inspiration that you have accumulated through your search into your own original image. After all, directly copying others is a clear lack of originality, not an increase of it. Your followers will recognize that and will fail to engage with your brand if you do not find a way to boost your originality and stay authentic on the platform.

Avoid Over Editing

Instagram leaves many striving to look professionally polished and well put together, and for a good reason — everyone else on the platform looks really incredible! When you edit your photographs properly, you can really make yourself pop against the rest of the photographs being shared, which means that you can get seen by even more people. As your target audience sifts through their favorite hashtags and discovery pages, chances are, they will be clicking a more attractive photograph over one that seems sloppy or out of place.

That being said, you need to be cautious about how much you are editing your photographs and what they look like in the end. If you edit your photograph too much, it will begin to look unnatural and even strange, which can result in fewer people paying attention to your page or taking you seriously. If you want to be taken seriously and increase your page engagement, you need to edit your photos tastefully and in a way that helps them stand out because they look *good,* not because they look strange from being overdone.

A great way to edit your photos and create a natural appeal while still having that professionally polished look to them is to use two apps on your phone: Lightroom CC and FaceTune Lite. Both of these applications are free and allow you to create professional, high-quality Instagram photographs in less than two minutes. Start by uploading your preferred image into Lightroom CC, going to the "light" setting, and then tapping "auto". The application will then automatically adjust settings such as the color hues, saturation, white balance, and black balance, and other settings to ensure that your photograph looks professionally edited. Next, if you want to, you can upload the image into Face Tune and soften the appearance of the skin of anyone in the image, as well as conceal any blemishes or perform any other minor adjustments to produce a high-quality appeal. Once again, this is where you really need to foster the belief that less is more. If you are whitening someone's teeth, for example, do not go too far: no one's teeth are incredibly white, so editing anyone's teeth to appear excessively white will make the picture look unnatural and uncomfortable. Make sure that every edit you make appears natural, even if it is meant to make the individual look like a professionally photographed model!

Favor Comments over Likes

The latest version of the Instagram algorithm prefers genuine engagement over passive engagement. Passive engagement, like "likes", is valuable, but it does not stand out in the algorithm to the point that Instagram believes that you genuinely want to continue engaging with the said person. So, if you "like" someone's picture, you still may not see very much of their content in your native newsfeed unless you like many of their pictures or comment on their pictures. The key here is that if you are seeing more of them in your feed, the chances are that they are seeing more of you in their feed as well, which means that you are more likely to be seen and engaged with by your own audience too.

When you are scrolling hashtags to locate new followers or conduct market research or to simply engage with your target audience, do your best to leave comments on everything along the way. That being said, do not leave ungenuine comments that are generic, and do not say the same thing on multiple photographs. In this day and age, there are programs called "bots" and most people will refuse to engage back with anyone whom they believe is a bot for fear of being spammed or scammed by others.

Furthermore, genuine comments stand out and often earn back engagement, which further increases your ability to get seen by that individual. For that person, they see you as authentic and are more likely to check you out and follow you on the platform. For Instagram's algorithm, the back-and-forth commenting suggests that you are sharing a genuine engagement and encourages Instagram's algorithm to show you higher in each other's feeds so that you can see each other's content more. As a brand or small business, this is exactly what you want happening so that you can stay relevant with your followers and increase your chances of being located and remembered by them.

Chapter 6: Choosing Your Niche

Having a niche on social media is extremely important, especially if you desire to make a strong connection with followers and attract a network of potential clients. As with any other form of business, a niche is good for one very specific thing: helping you know exactly whom you are talking to so that your audience knows when they are being talked to. In the marketing world, there is a saying: "If you speak to everyone, you will speak to no one." In other words, with marketing, there is no way to appeal to every single person in your marketing strategies, and since you likely do not have the team, time, resources, or reputation to create multiple different forms of marketing strategies to target everyone, you need to narrow down.

If you already run a business, you may have a niche carved out already. Or maybe you do have a business, but you have never needed to create a niche because your business is something like a car dealership which tends to have a broad range of people who are interested in what you are selling. In this case, you are going to need to choose an angle, which still requires you to have a niche or a target audience that you are selling to. In this chapter, you are going to learn how to identify a niche whether you already have a business but have not yet niched down, or if you are brand new and need to identify your niche.

Niching Down When You're Already in Business

If you are already in business, creating a niche is simple: you need to go through your recent sales records and get an idea of who is typically purchasing your products or services. Since you are already in business, you have the unique opportunity of being able to look at statistics that are relating to your actual paying clients, which makes it easier for you to decide exactly who you should be targeting online. This process should be easy for you, then.

If you find that you have two or three groups that primarily buy from you, you are going to want to identify which group is most likely to be on Instagram so that you can target them primarily. Then, you can incorporate the other two niches through smaller efforts in your marketing strategies. This is called the 80/20 or 60/20/20 rule, which essentially means that you give the larger portion of your marketing efforts to your main audience and then smaller one or two portions of your marketing efforts to your sub-niches. So, if you are a car dealership with a primary audience of families and you have a secondary audience of young couples, 80% of your efforts would go toward marketing to families, and 20% of your efforts would go to marketing toward young couples. If you had a third major sub-niche in there which constituted of single business folks, then you would divide it up by committing 60% of your marketing efforts to families, 20% of your marketing efforts to young couples, and 20% of your marketing efforts to single business folks.

You should never divide your efforts up more than three ways, as this can lead to you becoming confusing and difficult to follow as you have too many different messages running through your platform. If you have more than three audiences that you want to target, you need to decide which are going to be profitable and which are going to fit together the best for you in creating an overall image that makes sense. Avoid mixing together audiences that do not go together like young men who are looking for hot sports cars and older couples who are looking for safe sedans. These types of pairings make no sense together, and therefore, can make it challenging for your audience to know whether or not they want to follow you. In this exact scenario, you would rule out the elderly individuals who are looking for sedans because they will not be easily found on Instagram. Instead, you would put your Instagram efforts toward young men looking for sports cars and find a different way to connect with the elderly individuals looking for safe sedans.

What Do You Like and Whom Can You Serve?

If you do not have a niche defined yet because you are new in business, you need to decide right now whom you want to be targeting. If you are creating an actual business model, you want to incorporate this information into your business plan so that you have an overall strategy for how you are going to approach your business and generate success. If you are creating an online personal brand with the intention of building a loyal following so that you can eventually become an affiliate marketer, you may not need a massive business plan, but you should still have a general idea of what direction you are heading in with your business.

The first step in identifying your niche is brainstorming whom you can serve or whom you would most like to connect with through your business or brand. Think about things that are actually enjoying and interesting to you, as you do not want to be committing to anything that does not bring you joy for a long period of time. Not only will attempting to show up in a niche that does not interest you cause you to feel bored and disinterested with your brand over time, but it will also lead to your audience feeling that you lack passion and interest in your niche. When your audience can tell you are not interested in what they care about, they will not be interested in following you either because it will become blatantly obvious that your entire page is strictly created for profit and that you do not genuinely care about it. Even if you are only in it for profit, people want to see that the faces of the companies they run are passionate, interested, interesting, and enjoyable to watch and pay attention to. Otherwise, they are going to look elsewhere for someone who is, and they will likely believe that you are not capable of giving them anything they are interested in receiving.

After you have brainstormed several industries that you would be interested in serving, narrow your list down to one or two that you would be the most interested in being a part of. Consider the ones that you have already been interested in for a long time and that you will continue to remain interested in to avoid choosing something that you are highly passionate about *right now* but that you may lose interest in over time.

Validating the Quality of Your Niche

Once you have narrowed down your potential niche topics to a few topics of interest, you can start validating which niche topic is going to be the most likely to serve you in achieving your goals through your Instagram business. There are a few criteria that you are going to need to look into in order to determine whether or not your desired niche is sustainable and worthy of your attention. Those criteria include longevity, popularity, and profitability.

The purpose of looking into the longevity of a niche is to determine whether or not you are likely to be able to continue growing in that niche for a long period of time. You do not want to pick a niche that has peaked, or one that is attached to a trend that is going to fade out after some time as this will result in you not being able to create consistent growth over time. You can validate the longevity of a niche through a simple Google search. Pay attention to information such as: how valuable the industry is, how many people are in the industry, and how the industry is projected to do in the coming year(s). Then, pay attention to how your specific niche fits into that industry, how well it is progressing, and how much money is being spent on your unique niche. For example, the beauty industry was worth $445 billion in 2018, it grew by about $180 billion in one year, and it has billions of people involved in it. More specifically, the perfume industry, which is a sub-niche of the beauty industry, was worth $72 billion in 2018, it grew by about $3 billion in 2018, and it features millions of individuals interested in purchasing perfume. The projected growth rate for the perfume industry is about $3 billion per year for at least the next five years, which proves that the perfume industry would be a positive industry with excellent longevity for the years to come.

The next part of your niche that you need to consider is how popular that niche is. If you have done your due research, you should know whether or not your desired niche is popular. Ideally, your niche should have more than one million interested individuals if it is going to be popular enough to allow you to grow into it. Otherwise, it may be too small for you reasonably to grow into and profit from. Certain "ground level" niches, or brand-new industries that are just on the rise, may be worth getting into if you are educated in growing brand-new businesses and if you are ready to wait for the niche to grow over time. However, if you lack the skills and resources to build a brand-new business in an up-and-coming niche, you are better to wait until it grows in popularity or pick something else that is proven and reliable.

As you determine the popularity rating of your niche, do some research on what your niche's specific demographic is so that you can determine whether or not your target audience will even be on Instagram. If your primary objective is to get on Instagram and start making money, you do not want to do yourself a disservice by choosing a niche that will be popular but will not be large on Instagram, as this can lead to you wasting your time on Instagram.

Lastly, you need to decide how profitable your niche is going to be. Now, this is completely different from how profitable you can make it. Just because a niche is bringing in millions or even billions of dollars does not mean that you are going to be guaranteed to effectively tap into that flow and generate a decent profit off of it. However, you need to know that the ability to become profitable is there so that as long as you put in all the effort on your behalf, you can ensure that there is money to be made. This is simple: go back to the research you did to determine the size of your niche and see how large your niche is, and how much money is circulating in it every single year. If the profitability is up in the multiple millions of dollars range, you can confirm that your niche is likely profitable enough for you to stake a claim in that circulation and develop wealth through this niche. If the profitability is fairly high but seems to be dropping every year over multiple years, consider avoiding this niche as the chances are that it is losing popularity and is no longer a good opportunity for new people looking to come into the niche. Although you may be able to make some money before the niche dies off completely, it will result in you building into a position where you will need to rebuild once the niche becomes irrelevant. You do not want to waste your time doing that!

Finding Your Niche on Instagram

Lastly, you need to find your niche on Instagram! This is easy. Once you have your profile set up, simply go ahead and search some generic hashtags that relate to your niche. For example, search #yoga, #wellness, #lawyer, #realtor, or anything else broadly relating to your niche and start practicing the process of liking and commenting on the posts that come up in these areas. Right now, do not worry so much about getting found and followed as you do simply finding your niche and seeing how popular it is on Instagram. If you want, you can "Follow" these hashtags so that you can stay up to date with your niche online.

Finding and following your niche on Instagram this way is going to allow you to stay up-to-date on what is going on through Instagram with your niche. If you are in an industry where trends frequently come through, this will allow you to stay up-to-date with all of these trends so that you are never falling behind or becoming irrelevant through your business. Even if you are not, you may still be surprised to see how many new ways to market your business are introduced through these hashtags. It is never a bad idea to follow your market on Instagram and stay up-to-date so that you can remain informed on the best ways to use Instagram for your growing brand or small business.

Chapter 7: Positioning Your Brand

Positioning your brand on Instagram is your necessary action step in getting your brand's account in front of the people who need to see and interact with you and your products. When you are on Instagram, your goal is to make sales, so you need to be hanging out in the places where you are most likely to connect with people who are going to want to purchase from you or your company. This works by getting yourself in front of three primary audiences: your potential customers, your industry's influencers, and your primary competitors. When you spend time following and engaging with these three areas on the platform, you will leverage your ability to get found. From there, all you need to do is make your account stand out so that people who land on it realize that they have found something incredible and feel inspired to follow you and begin engaging with your brand on a more constant basis.

In this chapter, you are going to learn about what you need to do in order to position your brand so that you can get found and start leveraging Instagram for sales in minimal timing. The belief that you need to have thousands of followers to start making sales on Instagram, or anywhere else online for that matter, is a false belief that many people have when they first emerge into internet marketing. The truth is: as long as the right people see you, you can start making high-end sales, even if you only have a hundred plus followers, as long as you are creating the right content and getting that content in front of the right people.

Knowing Where to Spend Time on Instagram

Instagram offers many different opportunities to engage with followers and start creating a dynamic and interactive image for your brand so that when people find your profile, they have the opportunity to engage with you in many ways. Typically, most brands should be spending time on IGTV, stories, posting content, and engaging with other people's content. These four primary areas will give you the best opportunities to begin creating a massive impact in minimal timing.

Whenever you are marketing, particularly on the internet, you should ask yourself: what can I do that will gain me the most impact with the least amount of work possible? Ideally, you want to do one thing and have it make an impact in many different ways so that you can begin reaching people in a more impactful manner. We're going to

41

break down how you can use each of the four mentioned strategies to maximize your engagement and build your following fast, while also positioning your brand in the perfect place online so that your following is actually a part of your target audience. We are going to go deeper on how to use these to leverage your following and encourage people to follow you in Chapter 10: Grow Your Following, but here we are going to discuss how you can use these to make the most impact possible. If you really want to leverage these strategies, however, you will want to combine the process of making a massive impact with the process of making content that encourages people to follow you so that you can grow fast.

IGTV can be leveraged in one easy way — create a vertical video that provides immense value and lasts from three-ten minutes. As you do, consider how you can appeal to your following on Instagram, as well as any other platform that you may hang out on, such as Facebook and YouTube. Then, once your video is filmed, post it on IGTV and share that video to your other platforms so that other people who follow you on these platforms can find it and gain value from the video as well. You can also embed this video in e-mail newsletters so that people can locate you online and start following you in addition to receiving your newsletters. This way, one single video can have a huge impact on reaching your target audience online.

Stories give a more interactive behind-the-scenes opportunity for your fans to start seeing what your brand is really about and building a more intimate relationship with you and your company. You can leverage stories by simply snapping a few on-brand photographs throughout the day and sharing a word or two about what is going on in your life or the behind-the-scenes life of your brand. Another great way to leverage stories is to create small teaser films that give an even more interactive opportunity to see what you are up to and what is being created in your brand. Examples of effective story use would be Amanda Frances sharing thirty-second clips from her latest video trainings to encourage people to become interested and buy the official training programs, or Kylie Jenner sharing black and white videos of her new lip colors to build excitement.

Posts were the original way of sharing on Instagram, and they are still incredibly important when it comes to growing your brand online. Your Instagram posts are your opportunity to create a feed that looks aesthetically appealing, and that encourages people to want to follow you and pay attention to more of your posts. Typically, people are going to look for three things in your post: how attractive the image is, how relatable the caption is, and how much value the caption offers them based on what they are looking for. You can learn more about making aesthetically appealing posts with high-quality captions in Chapter 8: Creating Posts. When it comes to leveraging posts, the best way is simply to share these posts across different platforms. However, if you do this, make sure that you review the captions and that they are inclusive of other platforms. For example, if you have a caption that says, "Buy this at the link in my bio!" and you share the image to Facebook, your Facebook followers will not be able to find your "bio" since you are sharing it from a separate platform. For that reason, you will need to go over to your Facebook photograph and adjust the caption to provide the clickable link for people to be able to go to whichever link that you are seeking to have your followers visit. This way, you can allow your pictures to have a larger impact without making it seem like you are not being thoughtful or authentic across each platform, or leaving money on the table by having people interested but unable to find the link that you are referring to.

Lastly, engaging with other people, as you know, is one of the best ways to build engagement as this allows you to get seen by more people who are interested in stuff just like yours. When you engage with the right people, you can have a massive impact by being seen not only by the person that you are engaging with but also everyone who follows that individual. For example, you might notice that if you comment on a famous profile, you start getting several followers from other people who follow that particular account as well. You will notice this happening and can attribute it to those celebrity profiles and the comments you made because some of the followers you gain will be fan accounts of the initial account that you engaged with. While doing this and gaining followers from any random industry is not effective, you can leverage this as an opportunity to connect specifically with those in your industry by emphasizing your commentary engagement on famous profiles relevant to your industry. For example, if you are an astrologer, commenting on famous astrologer profiles and leaving genuine feedback or support is a great opportunity to get seen by other people who are paying attention to these accounts as well. That way, their followers see you and become interested in following you as well, which means that your comments not only help you engage with other accounts and get boosted in individuals' newsfeeds, but they also help you to get new followers. Furthermore, anyone who follows both you and these famous accounts will likely see your name and your comment when they are scrolling, as Instagram likes to show people what their friends are commenting on each other's profiles. So, any time they see this famous account on their newsfeed, they will also see your comment on the account which will remind them about you and your brand. Thus, these comments can be leveraged for far more traction than comments that are made on smaller accounts where the only person likely paying attention is the individual who owns the account.

Creating an Appearance People Want to Follow

When you are engaging with Instagram, it is imperative that you position your brand by creating a uniformed appearance that people actually want to follow. You need to make sure that the images and messages that you are sharing on your IGTV, stories, profile, and comments all reflect the same thing so that your brand remains consistent. When people can expect consistency out of your brand, they know that you are trustworthy and that you are a positive brand to engage with.

If you already have a brand in place, you likely have an idea of what consistency is and why it is important that your brand image and message remains consistent no matter where you are sharing. In this case, your goal should be to adapt that existing brand image to fit Instagram so that your profile remains true to the core values of your brand, but relevant to the core values of Instagram and the people who spend time on the platform. If you were to take your Instagram profile and place it next to any other profile that you have online or platform you use offline, the overall aesthetic and the messages should be consistent to show that you are the same brand that these individuals have come to know and love. That way, people can immediately recognize you, and they do not grow confused with who you are or what it is that you are offering because you are staying consistent across all of your platforms.

If you are a brand-new brand, you are going to need to create a general image that you can carry on Instagram so that you can remain consistent. The best way to do this is to create a mood board and a mission statement that you can use as the basis for everything that you are going to post on your platform. Mood boards or image boards that feature many different images, colors, and fonts, are used to generate an overall aesthetic for what you desire your brand to look like on Instagram. You can create a mood board on any photo editing platform like Canva or Pic Monkey, and use that mood board to "check" all of your images through. If your chosen images look like they fit in perfectly with your mood board, then you know that they will fit in perfectly with your website. If your chosen images look out of place, then you know that you are going to need to make adaptations to your photograph to ensure that it remains consistent with your overall aesthetic. The same can be done with your mission statement. If the post clearly resembles the core messages being offered in your mission statement, then you know that it will be on-brand and it will resonate with your target audience. If your post is not on-brand, then you know that you need to adjust it to ensure that it accurately reflects the values and mission of your brand.

Positioning Yourself as Being the Expert

The last thing you need to do in order to really position your brand online is to ensure that you are positioning yourself as the expert on the platform. You need to make sure that when people look at your account, they know that you are the go-to person because you clearly know what you are talking about and you can help them with what they desire to know more about. You can position yourself as the expert by using posts that exert authority, expertise, and credibility. Make it clear through your language, your message, and even your posture in your image, that you are someone who is confident and who clearly knows what you are talking about. This way, people can trust that what you are sharing with them is honest and that you are trustworthy enough for them to follow you and your message.

As you will learn in Chapter 8, one of the biggest mistakes that people make when they are on Instagram is creating posts that are flimsy or that lack true authority and credibility. You do not want to be posting things consistently that exclusively ask questions, nor do you want to be consistently posting things that make it sound like you do not know what you are talking about or like maybe you are not the person to trust with their needs. For example, if you are a financial advisor, talking about your own financial hardships may indicate that you are not trustworthy or that you are unable to handle finances well enough to handle your clients' finances effectively. However, if you are talking about troubles you had in the past and are effectively wrapping them up with a lesson that proves that these troubles were a part of your past and that you now know enough to help not only yourself but others as well, it may be worth talking about. Even still, you will need to be cautious about your wording to avoid making it seem like you are taking yourself out of a position of authority by giving away the fact that you did not use to be good at what it is that you claim to be the expert in now.

Chapter 8: Creating Posts

Your newsfeed makes up for about one-third of your sharing opportunities when it comes to putting your brand in front of your audience. The other two-thirds are split evenly between IGTV and Instagram stories, which both deserve to have just as much attention to detail as your posts do. In this chapter, you are going to learn how to create powerful posts that are going to support you in attracting new customers to your profile so that you can maximize your brand reach and exposure.

When it comes to posting on IGTV or stories, you should continue to follow the very same steps to ensure that all of your content remains consistent and on-brand. You will notice that in each area where we have discussed how you can create posts for your feed, we have also discussed how you can adapt those particular "rules" to create posts for your stories and IGTV as well. This way, you will be creating powerful content for all three areas where you have the best opportunity to get in front of your target audience and create meaningful and powerful content for those who are following you or those who have just found you.

The Main Ingredient: Your Images

The main ingredient of your posts on Instagram, no matter where you are sharing, is your image. Your images are the first thing that people are going to pay attention to when they land on your profile to determine whether or not they want to follow you, see more of what you have to offer, or otherwise engage with your brand. If you want to maximize your engagement, you need to create images that are going to stop people from scrolling, keep them paying attention to you for a few moments, and hopefully, result in them clicking through to your profile to learn more.

On your feed, your images all need to remain consistent and attractive. Most people will organize their images in a way that produces a "theme" or a consistent appearance throughout their profile so that they can have that aesthetically appealing image that people tend to look for on Instagram. You can create your own aesthetically appealing image on your feed by following your brand's mood board, as discussed in Chapter 7, as well as by creating your own theme and ensuring that your images fit perfectly into that theme. If you want a particular posting theme that creates a visual image, such as alternating between sharing quotes and then images or selfies, consider looking at your competition's profiles and see how they are designing their own feeds. This way, you can get a feel for what appearance you like the most, and what appearance your mutual audience likes the most; thus allowing you to create a theme that has a great impact.

Aside from ensuring that your photograph fits into the overall aesthetic of your feed and your brand, you also need to make sure that your photograph is high-quality. If you can, do some light editing on the image so that it still appears natural, but it creates a higher quality or more professional look to it. The nicer your images look, the more likely people will be to pay attention to your feed and choose to follow you, so it is certainly worth your time to create an image that looks highly appealing. If you are not a professional editor, recall the two applications mentioned previously that can be downloaded directly onto your phone. Lightroom CC and Face Tune Lite are both great apps that can be used to create natural looking edits without having to do too much work yourself. Remember: do not over-edit your images or they will begin to look strange, and people will not want to follow you because it will be clear that you are over editing your images; thus making you seem tacky and uninteresting. People like natural and authentic, even if it is minorly touched up to create a more appealing image overall.

Looking Through Your Audience's Eyes

When you are creating your posts, from your image to your caption, make sure that you look through your audience's eyes and consider what they are going to be seeing and picking up on through your posts. Your audience will typically pay attention to two primary things: how attractive they are and how much value they can gain from those posts in a small amount of time. This means that you need to be creating an image that is attractive and worthy of paying attention to, and a caption that offers immense value without it requiring too much time for your audience to gain that value.

Every single time that you begin to create a post, start by asking yourself what your audience would want to be seeing right now and what is relevant to what your audience is looking for. Then, as you go through the creation process, keep your audience in mind. Make sure that every single part of the post is created for them so that they are more likely to actually read and engage with what you have shared with them.

Taking, Finding, and Choosing Your Images

If you are building a branded account, you may be wondering just where you are going to get all of your images from! Considering the fact that you should be uploading between one and three images every single day, you might be overwhelmed by thinking that all of these pictures need to be taken and edited every single day. The reality is – they do not need to be taken daily, edited daily, or even taken by you in order to be used on your Instagram account. In fact, there are many ways that you can accumulate content for your account without having to plan daily photo shoots and edit the photos that you are taking for your profile.

There are typically four ways that people create content for Instagram: taking their own pictures, sharing pictures, using stock pictures, or creating quote pictures. Those four types of content will be explained in greater detail below, including how you can accumulate many of them for a low time investment.

Taking Your Own Pictures

Taking pictures does not have to be time-consuming or challenging. In fact, you do not even need to have any professional experience in handling cameras to start taking phenomenal photographs for your Instagram profile. The easiest way to start taking Instagram pictures is to think about your brand, consider what part of your daily life fits into your brand, and then take some pictures of that part of your day.

Another great way to accumulate photographs that are on-brand is to take extra photographs any time that you are in an environment that reflects your image. So, if you are a traveler, take several pictures when you are hiking, on planes, or eating at new restaurants so that you have a plethora of photographs to share on your profile. This way, you are not required to take new daily photographs or ensure that you are always in branded environments because you already have a reserve of photographs for you to use if you ever need them.

Sharing Pictures

On Instagram, a really powerful tool that brands can use is sharing other people's photographs. This is called using "user-generated content" which essentially means that you are using photographs that your followers took that relate to your brand in some way. Typically, brands will do this when one of their followers shares something and then tags their brand in it, as this is a great way to show their products or services being put to use by those around the world. You can see this happening with brands like Starbucks or Tim Hortons, where they use a lot of user-generated content to show off their coffees being enjoyed by fans everywhere. Early on, you may not be able to use much user-generated content, but as you continue to grow and work together with influencers, this will become easier for you to do.

Stock Pictures

Stock pictures are another great way to access photographs that you did not have to take yourself. There are plenty of royalty-free stock images out there to be used on websites like Unsplash or Negative Space, as well as paid ones that are available through platforms like iStock or Adobe Stock. You can decide whether or not you want to pay for your photographs, as there are benefits to both non-paid and paid photographs depending on what you are looking for. The obvious benefit of non-paid photographs is that they are free, which means that you can accumulate several of them and use them without having to worry about prices. However, royalty-free stock images tend to be used frequently which means that you are more likely to end up posting images that other brands have already used, making yours seem less original. Even so, you can still do this to curate an amazing feed, and for the most part, your followers likely will not mind. On the other hand, paid stock images are less likely to be used by the average population which means that if you pay for your stock photographs, you are less likely to have repeating images. As well, paid stock sites tend to have higher quality photographs and a much broader variety of photographs for you to use on your platform. You will need to decide which route offers you the most benefits and go from there to ensure that you are getting the best deal possible.

Quote Pictures

Another common form of an image that you will see on Instagram is quote photographs, which are best if you create them so that you can use your brand's colors and fonts, as well as add your logo if you desire. Quotes on Instagram should be used sparingly or at least balanced with photographs of faces; however, they do offer you the opportunity to add extra content and value for your audience. Plus, they are easy to create, do not require any intentional photo shoots, and can be shared across other platforms as well. You can easily use platforms like Canva or Word Swag to create quote images for your website, where each of these has both free and paid options for you to take advantage of depending on what you are looking for.

Getting the Message Across

When you are posting on Instagram, you are going to need to ensure that your message is written in a way that is actually tangible by the people who are paying attention to what you are posting. On Instagram, generally longer captions or overly wordy captions will not be interesting to the people whom you are trying to attract, so you are going to need to make sure that you take your time to find a way to say things with the least amount of words possible. For example, rather than saying, "We have a really great sale this weekend going on at our Vancouver location. You can find tons of hot prices on new shoes and handbags! Go to our website for a sneak peek of all the details!" you could say, "Sale @ Vancouver location this weekend! Shoes, Handbags, & More! Hit the #Linkinthebio for details!" This is clearly a lot shorter, gets to the point quicker, and ensures that your audience is more likely to follow through on your call to action of heading to your link because you have enticed their interest.

If you are planning on offering a message through video, you will need to consider what is the best way to do it. If you have a short message that will take under a minute, you can always offer that message through your story feed by quickly saying what you are thinking on a story image. Or, if you have a longer message to share, you can always share it through LIVE video if you don't mind it being deleted within 24 hours, or on IGTV if you want it to stay up longer. Alternatively, you might consider creating a short 60-second or less video and sharing it on your feed if it aligns with your image and will boost the look of your feed.

The big key with Instagram is always to keep your messages flashy and to the point. People on Instagram like to be wowed by the new content they are seeing and reading, so you need to stand out from the rest of the crowd. You need to keep things snappy, interesting, and relatable so that your audience will pay attention to you.

That being said, you also want to make sure that you are embedding enough value into your posts to make it worth reading and to make your call to action worth following. You can encourage people to read and gain that value by using the same language that your audience uses, describing things in a way that allows them to cognitively associate your brand with something, such as a feeling, and using call to actions that are both obvious and hidden. Yes, in many cases, hiding your call to action is a great way to ensure that it is in there, but that it does not stand out in a way that makes every single post seem like you are just trying to drive customers through your checkout process. You can embed a secret call to action by saying things like, "Aren't these cat eye sunglasses adorable?! Our designers really hit it out of the park with these ones!" which shows your audience that you are excited about the sunglasses that you just came out with. If they enjoy the sunglasses as well, they will be likely to go over to your page and see if they can find them through your link so that they, too, can own a pair of them.

Alternatively, you can use a different approach where you reference a program or service that you offer through a description you are sharing. In this scenario, you would offer a piece of free advice or information, reference a program where you offer similar information, and then conclude your point. For example: "3 Steps to Law of Attraction Success. We go deeper in my Manifestation Masterclass, but the core steps are:" and then you go on to offer those three steps. This gives the readers value right away and also references a program that you want them to check out if they desire more information on the subject. Through this type of call to action, you have created interest around your offer and embedded the idea of checking it out in your audience's mind without actually asking them to go see it. This way, people do not feel like they are being excessively advertised to through your page and they are much more likely to continue following you and checking out your offers.

Using Hashtags Effectively

Your hashtags are an extremely important element in your posts as they give you the opportunity to get seen by people who are not already following you and they increase your chances of getting seen by the ones who are. You need to use hashtags effectively in order to ensure that you are getting spotted by the people who need to be seeing your profile so that you can maximize your visibility, and as a result, maximize the number of followers that you can gain as well. There are two ways that you can find hashtags to help you start connecting more with your targeted audience. One way includes in-app research, and the other requires you to use a third-party application. Below, we will discuss both of these ways.

In-App Research

In-app research can be done on Instagram by searching up keywords relating to your niche and then going to their hashtag pages. For example, if you search "fitness" in the search bar and then go to the "#fitness" page, you will have the opportunity to start finding some great fitness-related hashtags for you to use on your profile. Once you land on the page for #fitness, you will find how popular that hashtag is, the photographs that have been linked to it, and similar hashtags that are being used by people on Instagram. Here, you want to do three things. If the hashtag you searched is extremely relevant to your niche, write it down and keep it in a document somewhere so that you can access it later. Then, go through the related hashtags and start clicking them to see how many followers they have. You want the majority of the hashtags that you will be using to have between 50,000 and 500,000 followers as this ensures that they are big but not so big that you are going to get buried underneath new posts if you use them. Typically speaking, hashtags with millions of photographs linked to them get new photographs every few seconds, meaning your photograph will be essentially buried by other photographs within just a few minutes. On the smaller ones, they are still being used and searched frequently, but they are not being used at such a high ratio, so you are less likely to get completely buried by your competitors.

Once you have written down all of these hashtags, you can start clicking through to the top posters who are using the hashtags on your list and see what else they are tagging in their photographs. Make sure that you find as many hashtags relevant to your niche as possible. You can use up to 30 hashtags per post, and you do not want to use the same ones over and over again, or you will find yourself struggling to reach new audience members. Instead, you should be shaking it up by using between 60-120 hashtags that you can change on every single post to ensure that you are always targeting new areas of your audience.

Third-Party Applications

Third-party applications are another great way to find hashtags relevant to your business and use them for your posting. Apps like

PLANN and Iconosquare have in-app features that allow you to research the hashtags that are relevant to your business and compile them in lists that can be used whenever you are posting on your Instagram page. For these applications, you simply type in a keyword that is relevant to your business or industry, and there will be a list populated with several hashtags or similar hashtags that you can use for your photographs. PLANN, in particular, is a great app because it offers specs on its lists that show you how frequently the hashtags are being used. Hashtags that are highlighted in green are used in a reasonable amount of time, ensuring that your picture is likely to be seen, and hashtags highlighted in dark blue or red are used too frequently and should be avoided. The lighter blue color signifies that the hashtag is not used often, although if it is used more than 50,000 times, you should still consider using it to help your picture get seen more frequently.

Using Hashtags Correctly

Depending on where your picture is being posted will ultimately depend on how you are using hashtags. If you are posting your hashtag on your page, you should write your hashtags out in a note and copy them before posting your picture so that you can immediately post them in the first comment on your image. You want to do this instead of posting them in the caption with your written text because this way, your caption stays clean and separate from your hashtag list. Some people will use multiple dots and enter spaces to put their hashtags lower in the caption section, but this looks messy and distracting and can take away from the professional image on your page. By putting them in the comment section, your picture remains attractive and professional.

If you are posting a story, you can also use one to two hashtags in your story to help it get seen by the people who are following certain stories. This way, your story is likely to get seen by more than just your following audience, which means that you actually add an additional way for you to be located through Instagram! You may also use hashtags in the descriptions of live videos and IGTV videos to help get found, although they may not be quite as effective on these platforms, so only use a couple to avoid having them overwhelming the descriptions.

Creating a Posting Schedule

On Instagram, it can be extremely helpful to create a posting schedule that determines when you are going to post on Instagram. The biggest benefit of posting schedules is that you can align them with your most popular activity times on Instagram to ensure that your posts are getting as much traction as possible right away, which helps them gain more long-term traction as well. Another great benefit of using a posting schedule is the fact that once you have a schedule, you know exactly when you need to post every single day, so there is no guessing or trying to fit it into your daily schedule. You simply pencil it in based on when your most popular time is.

The best way to create a posting schedule is to look into your Instagram business analytics or your third-party app analytics, both of which will tell you the optimal posting times for your account. For the first three to four weeks, post randomly throughout each day with no specific schedule, but instead aiming to try out new posting times each day. This way, your app has great diversified information to draw from to ensure that the analytics it curates for you are accurate to what posting times are popular for your account. Once you have your best posting times accumulated in your analytics graphs, you can start posting based on these schedules.

If you really want to leverage your analytics and posting schedule, start engaging with your followers and some of the hashtags that you will be using on your post about an hour before you actually post. You should be engaging periodically throughout the day, but by increasing your outgoing engagement at this time, you increase the popularity of your profile, which means that Instagram will be more likely to show your new post to the people whom you are engaging with. In other words, Instagram's algorithm thinks "you two were just interacting and having a conversation on another post. I'll bet this person will be interested in seeing your new post!" Of course, Instagram's algorithm does not have human-like thoughts, but this gives you an opportunity to understand how the algorithm's if-this-then-that (IFTTT) technology works so that you can begin leveraging it for greater popularity on the platform.

Minimizing Posting Time

Lastly, if you do not want it to take a long time for you to get your posts live on Instagram, there are a few ways that you can minimize posting time to ensure that you are not spending hours every single day engaging and creating posts so that you can connect with this segment of your audience. The best way to minimize your posting time is to use a scheduler, such as the ones through PLANN or Iconosquare, or even just creating posts and saving them as drafts. You can create a few days' worth of content in advance, including images, captions, and hashtags and then have them auto-post throughout the day. Or if you have them saved as drafts, you can set a reminder on your phone and go onto your app and launch the post when your reminder goes off. If you do this and you choose to keep your hashtags separate in the comments, make sure that you have reminders on your phone so that you can go to the app and copy and paste a set of hashtags into your latest post to ensure that it actually gets seen. After all, there is no point putting in the effort to schedule out posts only to fail to add your hashtags and have them seen by virtually no one!

Chapter 9: Gauging the Competition

On Instagram, the growing trend of small business users being on the platform also means that there is a growing number of competitors who are going to be using the platform alongside you. Some people in your niche will leverage the platform effectively and successfully gain new followers and customers through it, and others are going to struggle and ultimately fail to leverage the platform and find themselves spinning their tires. You, obviously, want to be amongst the first group of people who are actually creating success and advancing through the "ranks" on Instagram so that you can gain maximum followers and create a massive impact through your account.

Part of really growing your account and having success through Instagram is by knowing how to gauge your competition and leverage the information that you gain through your "spying" to increase your growth. The steps in this chapter are going to show you how you can ethically follow and spy on your competition and leverage their growth and information for the benefit of your growth.

Finding Your Competitors on Instagram

The first step is finding your competitors on Instagram, which is not terribly challenging to do! You will find your competitors the same way that you find your followers, since like you, your competitors are going to want to be spending a lot of time around your mutual audience. A great way to find your competitors is to go to your niche-specific hashtags and start looking at the people who are "liking" the posts that are being shared. Those "likes" will include businesses who are targeting the same audience as you, so all you need to do is scroll through them and identify the individuals who are clearly running business pages and start scrolling through their content. Now, it is up to you how you want to do this. You can follow your competitors, or you can simply make a point of revisiting their pages on a regular basis. Typically, it is easier just to follow your competitors so that you can see them in your newsfeed and stay up-to-date with what they are doing in an easier way.

Ideally, you want to be following around 10-15 of your competitors so that you can see a healthy range of your competitive audience. Make sure that you are following competitors who are where you are in business, as well as ones who are slightly ahead of you, and ones who are already where you desire to be with your business. This way, you can see a healthy array of what is working at every single stage in business, and you can start adapting the effective strategies of each stage into your methods so that you can aim for growth right off the bat.

Ethically Spying on Your Competitors for Inspiration

When you spy on your competitors for inspiration, the key is to make sure that you do not do it in a way that seems shady or hidden. On Instagram, the easiest way to do this is to engage with your competition and genuinely build relationships with them too. Instagram is a social community, and by doing so, you are showing that you are hoping for positive results for everyone in the industry, not just yourself. You can like and engage on other people's photographs who are a part of your competition, as long as you are not posting anything sleazy that seems as though you are trying to steal away their audience. For example, if you are an eco-friendly brand and your competitor posts new eco-friendly straws, instead of posting "Sweet, we just got these in too!" post "We love these too!" This way, you are showing support, but you are not blatantly trying to take away their audience and turn eyes over to your page.

Additionally, if you get inspiration from your competition, make sure that you adapt it in a way that suits your brand and does not make it appear as though you are going out of your way to copy them strategy for strategy. You do not want to completely mimic what another brand is doing or copy another brand directly as this makes it obvious that you are copying and makes your brand seem inauthentic and like it may be a scam or a fraud instead of a true brand. You want to make sure that you gain inspiration from others and that you put that toward creating your own unique approach instead, as this allows you to leverage new strategies while still remaining authentic to your brand.

Another powerful way that you can spy on your competitors and gain more information than what is just on the surface is by taking "Sneak Peeks" through apps like PLANN. These apps allow you to type in your competitors' usernames into a search bar and they show you your competitors' most popular images, hashtags, and their color palettes so that you can get a better snapshot of your competitors' brands. This is a great way to get in-depth inspiration for leveraging your competition's success to create your own!

How to Use the Information that You Find

The best way to take the inspiration that you gain from your followers and put it to work in your brand is to spend some time each week looking at your competitors' profiles and getting a sense for what they are doing when it comes to marketing. Pay attention to their latest trends, what they are saying, what their most popular posts are, and what new sales or offers they have going on in their business in that week. This way, you can accumulate the information on a regular basis and start putting it together so that you can incorporate it into your marketing strategies.

Once you have identified the trends and new strategies being used, you can go ahead and start highlighting the trends that seem to be working or drawing more attention to your competitor's profile. Then, consider how you could use those strategies in your business so that it aligns with your audience and your brand while still giving you the opportunity to leverage the growth and success of these new strategies. For example, if your competitor has been uploading more quotes recently and you notice that these quotes are gaining attention, you can start uploading more quotes to your profile as well. However, make sure that you are not directly copying the same quotes from the page that your competitor is using; instead, try to use original quotes that reflect your brand and image without appearing as though you are directly copying your competition. This way, you can start maximizing your growth through the strategies that are working for your competition, without coming off as a copycat or a rip-off brand.

Chapter 10: Grow Your Following

Perhaps the most important part of being on Instagram is growing your following so that you can actually have an audience to market to! Although every other part of this book has in one way or another contributed to your ability to grow your following and increase your outreach, there are still several things that you can do to really grow your Instagram account and start seeing higher engagement rates. In this chapter, you are going to discover what it takes to grow your following and start generating success through your Instagram account.

Encouraging Engagement on Your Page

The first thing that you can do to start increasing your following is to encourage people to engage with you on your page. Remember, the Instagram algorithm favors when people engage on others' pages, which means that if you can get your followers to start engaging with you more, you can feel confident that they are going to start seeing more of your content too. You can encourage engagement in two different ways: engaging with others and asking for engagement from your followers.

When you engage with the people who follow you on a regular basis, they feel more inclined to engage with you on your posts because they begin to feel the development of a relationship. The back-and-forth support between you and your audience becomes a regular part of your relationship. When you go out of your way to go through your follower list and start engaging with people, you actually "break the ice" between yourself and them, which makes them feel more comfortable and engaged with you and your brand. You can do this by regularly going through your list of followers and tapping on random accounts and engaging with their content. Leaving a few heartfelt comments and liking some of their recent posts is a great opportunity to start engaging with people and inspiring them to engage back with you the next time they see your content.

As you post, you can also ask for engagement by saying things like, "We love summer! Do you?" which encourages people to say, "Yes" or answer something on your profile picture. You can also increase engagement by writing captions that say things like: "Comment your favorite ____!" or "Tag a friend who would love this too!" Asking your followers to engage with your content in this way helps them break their thought process from mindless scrolling and choose to engage in your content instead.

Another great way to encourage engagement is to run giveaways on your page, which allows you to set rules that require individuals to engage with your post in order to enter in the giveaway. Often, companies will decide on what it is that they want to giveaway and then they will set the requirements for individuals to enter as something like, "Follow us, tag a friend, and share this post to your stories in order to be entered in the giveaway!" Then, they will leave the giveaway up for a certain period of time, allowing them to experience plenty of engagement from their followers. This type of behavior drives up engagement on that one post, but will also support you in driving up engagement on the rest of your posts as well. You obviously do not want to be engaging in too many giveaways, but two to four giveaways per year are plenty, and this is a great way to get engaged with more followers.

Regularly Updating Your Following List

The people and the hashtags whom you follow are the ones that populate your main home screen, which allows you to see images that everyone you are following shares on a regular basis. You want to ensure that you are regularly updating your following list so that you are only seeing people who reflect those that are actually associated with your branding or positioning. You might feel inspired to follow personal interests on Instagram, but this is typically best reserved for private personal accounts instead of business accounts. You want to ensure that your time spent scrolling through your followed accounts is spent investing in the growth of your business so that your scrolling becomes productive in the long run.

You can update your following list by going through and first unfollowing anyone who does not make sense to your brand. This way, you are not seeing content that is completely irrelevant to you or following accounts who are unlikely to provide you with any return on your engagement. You can only follow or unfollow up to 60 accounts in an hour, so take your time with this and do it regularly so that you do not have many changes to make to your account. You should be doing this on a weekly basis so that you are staying relevant in your industry and seeing the latest trends and people who are coming up.

Once you have unfollowed everyone who is not relevant to you, you can start going to your most popular hashtags and see if there are any new hashtags or followers for you to pay attention to through the top posts in these searches. This way, you can start following new users who may support you in bringing more attention to your account each time you engage with their content or interact with them. Plus, when you follow new hashtags that are trending in your niche, you can also go ahead and start using those hashtags on your photographs so that you can stay relevant as well. This type of research creates two powerful opportunities for growth in one move, so it is definitely worthy of your regular attention and time!

Saying the Right Thing at the Right Time

On Instagram, you really need to make sure that you are saying the right thing at the right time. By posting the right content at the right time, you can ensure that you stay relevant and that your content relates to what your audience is going through or thinking about so that your audience will be likely to pay attention to and engage with your content. The easiest way to say the right thing at the right time on Instagram is by following your audience and paying attention for latest trends, concerns, and issues that may be arising that people are paying attention to. For example, if you are in the blogging industry and you blog about current events in relation to famous people, you would want to be staying up-to-date on all of the latest trends and gossip and blogging on them as soon as they reach your eyes. The same would go for any industry you are in. The moment you see a trend or topic waving through your industry, you need to be prepared to get on board with it, customize how you share it according to your unique brand, and offering it as soon as possible.

In addition to following unexpected trends that rise in your industry, you also need to be following expected trends like holidays or scheduled events that are relevant to your audience. For example, if you are in the fashion industry, you should be paying attention to popular fashion events like Fashion Week and the Victoria Secret Fashion Show. If you are in the tech industry, you should be paying attention to the latest device launches and information regarding events that are big in the tech industry, like the annual E3 event. These types of events occur on a consistent basis, and they are extremely helpful in allowing you to stay relevant in your industry by paying attention to the information being released by those who drive the industry like influencers and developers.

It is important that you avoid talking about things out of season or out of turn, as sharing information too long after the event occurred can result in you coming across as irrelevant or outdated. Typically, people who see companies sharing outdated information will believe that this company is not paying attention or does not actually care enough to stay in the loop with what is going on in their industry. As a result, people simply will not follow you.

Remember, we live in the digital age where information can become available fast, and trends can rise and fall even faster. You need to be ready to get into these trends and start creating your brand's name in the heat of the moment and not after the trend or information has already started declining in popularity. If you find that staying on-trend is harder than it looks, try finding three to four people or blogs to follow who are always quick to jump into new trends and solely pay attention to these individuals or resources. This way, you are not overwhelming yourself by trying to follow too many people at once and becoming lost in what is relevant, what is actually a trend, and what is completely irrelevant to you and your audience.

Targeting Your Audience Through Your Words

You now know that Instagram's biggest way to target audiences is through hashtags, as this is how you can reach new audience members and start growing your audience fast. However, there is another verbal element that comes into play when it comes to creating an impact through your captions and writing – and this is by having words in your captions that actually resonate with your audience. You do not want to be using words that do not make sense to your audience or that sound completely irrelevant or outdated, as this will lead to your audience becoming disinterested in reading what you have to say and struggling to actually "follow" what you are trying to tell them.

The best way to speak like your audience is to pay attention to what they care about by following them back and listening to how they are speaking. Regularly scroll through your feed and actually read what the people you follow are saying so that you can get a feel for what their language is like, how they tone their messages, and if there are any unique slang words, phrases, or acronyms that they are using to connect with their audiences. The more you read your niche's own captions and comments, the more you are going to become familiar with how they are speaking, what they are saying, and what they are reading. This way, you can begin emulating their language through your own posts and saying things in a way that makes sense to your audience.

When you do start emulating your audience, there are a few things that you will need to refrain from doing to avoid having your audience tune out from what you are saying. The big thing is that you need to avoid emulating your audience to the point that you lose your authenticity because you sound like you are identical to those whom they are already reading. Make sure that you pay attention to your brand's voice and your mission statement and adapt the industry's language to meet your tone and not the other way around. If your tone seems too off-base for your industry, you can consider casually adjusting it slightly to fit the industry's needs more, but do not begin changing your approach too frequently or you will come across as fake and untrustworthy.

The second thing that you need to avoid doing is creating messages that are filled with industry jargon that your general following is unlikely to understand. If you attempt to use industry jargon that is commonly used between those who sell product and service in the industry, but that is unlikely to be recognizable by those who purchase in or follow the industry, you may lose your following solely because they do not understand you. You do not want to be creating gaps and confusion in your marketing by using language that your audience does not understand because this can make it unnecessarily challenging for people to follow you and support your business. Keep it simple, speak in a way that your audience will understand, and adapt the industry language to suit your brand's message and purpose.

Leveraging Instagram Stories

Instagram stories are a powerful tool that can be used to not only nurture your existing following but also attract new followers into your business. When you use your Instagram stories correctly, you can create a significant influx of engagement from your followers, add a personal opportunity to connect with your brand and create a more interactive page overall. On Instagram, people love interacting with the brands that they love and consuming as much of their content as they can, and Instagram offers plenty of ways for followers to do just that. As you upload stories throughout the day, you create the opportunity for your followers to feel like you are genuinely thinking about them throughout the day, which establishes a connection of care and compassion between you and your followers. Not only will this help you maintain your existing followers, but it will also help new or potential followers see how interactive and intimate you are with your following, which leads to them wanting to be a part of your following as well!

The reason why stories work is simple – people are nosy, and they like to know insider's information. This is not a bad thing either, but rather just a simple human experience where we all desire to be a part of something bigger than ourselves, and we want to connect with those around us to become a part of that "something bigger". You can position yourself as the facilitator of that "something bigger" by turning your brand into an experience that people can enjoy, and an entity that they can share an intimate and compassionate relationship with. Stories give you a great option to do that because every picture or short clip you share reflects a part of your personal behind-the-scenes experiences. You can also curate your story feed to offer an even more exclusive and intimate feel by purposefully sharing things that will allow others to feel like they are genuinely connected with you through your feed.

The key with making your stories intimate and leveraging them to attract new followers and maintain your existing ones is to make sure that the content you share in your stories is exclusive and unlike anything that you are sharing anywhere else. Be very intentional in sharing things that are more personal and "private" than what you would share on IGTV or on your feed itself because this way people feel like they truly are getting that private insight into your brand. Instagram stories are already somewhat exclusive because, after 24 hours, they are gone and cannot be viewed again. You can play up that exclusivity by sharing the right content, mentioning things that you shared stories about previously which new followers can no longer see, and even by mentioning outright that your story feed is exclusive. Say things like, "Keep your eyes on my stories because I'll be announcing an exclusive offer here first... Get it three days early just by watching the story!" or something similar.

The last way that you can really leverage Instagram stories is by making story highlights which can enable your new followers to see exclusive tidbits of your previous stories. So, if you are someone who regularly travels and you often share intimate travel experiences with people, such as the restaurants you dine at or the people you meet, you might consider sharing these in your stories. Then, you can create highlights of certain moments from your travels that were most exciting or interesting so that your new audience can glance back through your stories and start feeling more intimately connected with you right away. Leveraging your highlight reels in this way is a great opportunity to show your new followers what to expect, give them that feeling of having known you and your brand for a long time already, and increase their interest in you right from the start.

Using IGTV to Increase Your Following

IGTV is a great way to increase your following, as these videos stay in place for as long as you leave them up, meaning that followers can look back through your IGTV channel and watch stuff that you put up days, weeks, months, or even years ago once it has been around long enough. You can leverage IGTV to create new followers by creating excellent IGTV videos and then promoting them elsewhere on the net so that people are more likely to click over to your channel and watch. Once they see your video and the quality of the content you create, they can choose to follow your page to get more if they decide that they like you.

The big key opportunity with IGTV is that you can promote your IGTV channel just like you would a YouTube channel or any other free video content on the net. By creating great content and then sharing it around the net, you can encourage individuals to go over to your Instagram in order to be able actually to see the video. This means that you can funnel people from Facebook, Twitter, Snapchat, e-mail, and any other social media platform that you may be on to Instagram so that they can catch your free content and learn from it.

To make your content popular, you need to make sure that the IGTV videos you make are worthy of receiving views. In other words, you need to create high-quality, interesting, and relevant content that your audience actually wants to pay attention to so that when you share it to other platforms, they are more likely to click through to your channel and actually watch the content that you created. The best way to create valuable content is to offer entertainment, insight, or guidance in relation to your industry so that your audience is more likely to pay attention to it and watch it. For example, if you are an astrologer, you can create daily videos offering the astrological forecast for the day. If you are a sports announcer, you can create a daily video that highlights the most memorable sports moment of the week, or the latest stats of popular players or teams based on the sport that you announce for. If you are an educator of sorts, you can create a simple ten-minute or less tutorial on how your audience can do something for themselves that ties into your industry or your area of expertise. By creating valuable content like this, you make it easier for your audience to understand why and how they are gaining value from your IGTV which means that you will have an easier time promoting it and actually getting traction from that offer.

Once you have created amazing content, make sure that you leverage it in every way that you possibly can. Share it across all of your other social media platforms, talk about it in your stories, write about it in your latest post, and make sure that you save it for a future date. If you create timeless content, you can always reference back to older videos when a few weeks or months have passed so that you can use them as a marketing opportunity all over again. For example, if you are a make-up artist and you did a certain tutorial, you can promote the video as soon as you make it, then reference back to it if you notice someone famous wore a similar look in a recent event. This is a great opportunity to create one piece of content that has maximum impact, meaning that you can gain even more followers just from one excellent time investment. When it comes to marketing, that's really what it's all about!

Leveraging Influencers the Right Way

Brands and influencers go hand-in-hand, as they are both responsible for helping to generate success for the other. If you are not yet aware, influencers are individuals who build a trusting following in a certain industry and then advertise for industry-specific brands to their existing audience. A great example of an influencer, or a family of influencers rather, would be the Kardashian-Jenner-West family which is known for becoming and staying famous for a reason that most people cannot understand. This is because this particular family blew up around the same time that influencers were becoming a thing and they leveraged their star power to begin making brand deals and endorsing companies. At this point, most individuals in the family have their own businesses as well, although they still make money by endorsing other products and marketing these products to their respective audiences.

Influencers are solely focused on generating a massive following of people who like and trust them in a specific industry that interests them most and then marketing to their following for the products and companies that they like. As a brand, you can leverage influencers from your industry by having them test out your products or services and market them to their audience. Since their audience is already established and trusting in the influencer, you can trust that once the influencer has tried and endorsed your products, your own recognition and sales will increase as well.

The key here is making sure that you are working with influencers correctly. On Instagram, there is an unfortunate trend of companies that are attempting to work together with influencers and who are going about it in the wrong way, which results in them losing a lot of money in this area of potential growth. These companies, not knowing that they are making such drastic mistakes, find themselves attempting to work together with low-quality influencers, or individuals who are not yet true influencers, which results in them not making a massive impact. Rather than having their products in the hands of people who can actually make a difference, they are attempting to get their products into the hands of people who do not truly have an impact on their target audience. Typically, they will do so by encouraging potential "influencers" to buy their products and then make money any time their following purchases the products. In the end, the biggest way that the company is making money is by having the would-be influencers buying products and not through them actually marketing the products to their target audience. When companies use this method, they end up looking spammy and careless, which results in them being seen as low-rate companies that are not worthy of being trusted or invested in. In the long run, this leads to an unsustainable practice which can also lead to the premature demise of a company that could have otherwise succeeded in the online space.

If you really want to leverage influencers, you need to make sure that you are getting your products or services into the hands of people who can actually have an impact on your growth because they are already so connected with your target audience. Although you may lose some money by giving products away for free to these influencers, you will ultimately end up gaining money because they will drive a lot of traffic to your page and to your website. To create this positive and effective momentum in your business, you need to ensure that you are plugging into deals with the right influencers. Be very intentional and cautious about whom you offer your products or services to and make sure that every single influencer you work together with can truly make a positive impact on your business. As well, approach them professionally through their messages or email if they provide one, and not through their comments section on their photographs as this also comes across as unprofessional and spammy. If you want your company to look poised, respectful, and worthy of trusting and investing in, you need to make these long-term investments properly.

Increasing Your Posting Visibility

When you are posting on Instagram, you want to make sure that your posts are actually getting seen so that you can maximize your visibility, engagement, and traction overall. Instagram's algorithm favors individuals who get a lot of traction on their posts quickly and will ensure that even more people see these posts by placing it in more favorable viewing spots. If you want to gain these more favorable viewing spots, there are a few things that you can do to maximize your posting visibility and earn more followers overall.

As you already know, a posting schedule is a valuable way to start increasing your posting visibility because it enables you to be put at the top of search feeds around the same time that your audience would be looking for your types of posts. You can also ensure that you are engaging with other people before you post so that you appear higher in their newsfeed with your new posts as well.

Another way that you can increase your posting visibility is by choosing hashtags that are only used 300,000 times or less overall, as these ones make it easier for you to be posted in the "top posts" section of the hashtag. Most people will browse these posts first, so being seen in this section ensures that you are going to be seen more frequently by people in your target audience.

Another way that you can increase visibility is by creating high-quality posts and posting them consistently between one-three times per day. The more you post, the more you will be seen, and if your content quality is higher, people are going to continue following you and paying attention to your page. When you do post, follow all of the strategies in Chapter 8 to ensure that you are creating content that people actually want to pay attention to and engage with. Never post a photograph that is too low quality, as this will result in you having fewer followers or people unfollowing you because they may think that your quality is going down. You may notice that larger influencers and brands do occasionally post lower quality photographs, and the reason why they can get away with this is easy. They have a huge following already, and they are unlikely to be impacted by one image. You, however, can be impacted early on in a massive way. You want to avoid having people think that you are in any way posting low-quality content as this can lead to you losing credibility and then losing followers.

Lastly, if you want to really maximize your visibility, make sure that you are engaging specifically with the people who are following you. These are the individuals who are already seeing you in their own newsfeeds, which means that they are the ones who will be most likely to engage with you quickly when you post new content. If you can get your existing following to engage quickly, it will be easier for new followers to find you in their discover pages or on the top post tabs, which again makes it more likely for you to be discovered and followed by your target audience.

Engaging with Your Followers

That brings us to our next step: engaging with your followers! This is a great way to maintain your existing following, but it is also a great way to discover new people who will want to follow you. Think of it this way: your existing following is already a part of your target audience which means that they likely connect with people who are a part of your target audience also. By going to your followers' pages and connecting with them through their content, you establish a greater connection with your following which is also increasing your ability to be found by their followers and friends. When their audience sees you commenting on their posts, if they are interested in what your brand has to offer, they may then click through to your page and locate you. So, not only will this improve the way the algorithm works in your favor, but it will also add another avenue for people to discover you on Instagram.

Another way that you can leverage your existing following to gain more followers is to go to your followers' pages and click onto pictures that are relevant to your industry. For example, if you sell bikes and your follower posts an image of them mountain biking on a cross-country trail, this would be relevant to your industry. You can then look at the list of everyone who has liked this picture and begin engaging with these individuals by going to their pages, liking their content, commenting on a couple of pictures of theirs that you like, and then following that individual. This shows genuine interest, helps you stand out to that individual, and increases their chances of following you back. Of course, Instagram only allows 60 new follows or unfollows per hour, so make sure that you leverage this tool carefully to avoid being seen as spammy or overwhelming to the algorithm or your audience.

Once these new individuals follow you, your process of going through your followers and engaging with their content will further support you in maintaining and building your following because it makes it clear that you care. If you engage with someone just to earn their follow and then never engage with them again, people will start to see your brand as superficial which can result in them unfollowing you or no longer engaging with your content. Keep yourself genuine and connected as much as you reasonably can so that you are always building better relationships with your existing audience and new relationships with your potential audience.

Lastly, anytime your audience connects with you by commenting on your pictures, replying to your stories, or messaging you, make sure that you engage back with that individual. This shows that you genuinely care about them and what they have to say, and creates a positive relationship between you and that individual. Take some time out of your day each day to respond to all of these forms of engagement to make sure that you are really investing in building a meaningful audience. On Instagram, which revolves around its social experience, a little bit of returned engagement can go a long way in regards to building lifetime fans and relationships with your audience.

Analyzing Your Results to Increase Your Growth

Finally, you need to make sure that you are analyzing your results on Instagram to encourage greater growth on the platform! You can analyze your results either through the in-app analytics provided through Instagram itself or through a third-party application – if you choose to use one of those. You can do this however you feel most confident, as long as you are regularly checking in to see how your content is performing. By regularly checking in, you can ensure that you can clearly track trends in what your audience likes most, what content gets the best engagement, and what earns the most likes on your page. As you track these trends, it becomes easier for you to understand what types of pictures, content, and offerings your audience likes the most, which means all you need to do is start creating more of that type of content for your page.

Your analytics are not only going to support you in discovering what type of content you need to be creating for your page, but it will also help you determine what you should be creating and offering more of for your audience. These numbers will tell you exactly what products or services your audience enjoys most and what they are buying the most of, which allows you to begin offering more products or services in alignment with what your audience likes the most. If your business is solely on Instagram, you can create offerings that are specific to your Instagram audience and simply focus on expanding in the area that your Instagram audience seems to like most. If your business exists on several platforms, then you can pay attention to your analytics across all platforms and incorporate this into all of your future offers. If you find that the analytics vary from platform to platform, consider creating a variety of offers and then selling the offers that sell best on each platform exclusively on that platform. So, if you are a computer technician and you find that Instagram individuals seem to be more interested in purchasing tech products and accessories from you and Facebook individuals seem to be more interested in buying your actual services, you can market respectively. Any time you have a new product available, place the emphasis of your marketing around that product on Instagram and market only slightly on Facebook. Then, whenever you have a service to offer, place the emphasis of your marketing for that new service on Facebook and only reference it a few times on Instagram. This way, both audiences know that there is more to your business than what you are sharing exclusively on that platform, but you are not bombarding either audience with content that they do not typically pay attention to.

The last part of your analytics that you need to pay attention to in order to ensure efficient growth is how your audience on Instagram is relating to your actual target audience. On Instagram, a few accidental mistakes can lead to your audience being completely off the target, which can lead to you having a great sized following that is filled with people who are not actually interested in purchasing anything from you or your company. If you notice that your target audience and your Instagram audience are completely misaligned, or that your Instagram audience seems to engage with your content but never actually purchases anything, you need to start addressing your strategy. You want to make sure that you are putting your emphasis onto the parts of your audience that are actually going to support your conversion ratios by becoming paying clients; otherwise, your time spent on Instagram will be pointless.

If you do find that you do not have the impact that you desire to have, go back to the beginning of this book and start reviewing the chapters where we discuss carving out your niche and finding your audience on Instagram. Refreshing yourself on this information and moving forward with a renewed perspective can support you in actually connecting with the people that you mean to connect with, such as those who want to pay for your products or services!

Chapter 11: Selling on Instagram

Selling on Instagram takes place over three simple steps: creating sales funnels, marketing to the people who are most likely to pay you, and using display ads to reach those people effectively. In this chapter, we are going to explore these three selling opportunities and how you can leverage them to maximize your conversions through the Instagram platform.

While there are many ways to word your sales copy and many areas to post to on Instagram, there are generally three ways that you are going to be able to find followers who actually want to pay for your products. Sales funnels are the first one, and they are used to drive people around your profile in a methodical way that ultimately results in them clicking on your link and purchasing products that you have already built their interest in online. These are the easiest ones to create, but they do take some practice as it can be challenging to know how to smoothly drive people around your profile through your stories, posts, and IGTV videos. The second way that you can sell on Instagram is by drawing people into your actual storefront if you have one through local marketing. The rest of this book has been dedicated to locating global clients, so we are going to emphasize solely on attracting local clients if you are running a brick and mortar business in your city. Finally, display ads are another great way to sell as they make it clear that there is actually something for sale in the first place. You can use display ads as either posts or stories, depending on what your budget is and where you feel you are going to get the most traction from your ads.

Creating Sales Funnels on Instagram

Since Instagram offers plenty of opportunities to connect with your followers, it is easy for you to build Instagram into your sales funnel and start creating a higher conversion ratio through your account. Building your Instagram sales funnel will take some planning as you need to ensure that every channel on the platform is driving people through a "funnel" until they ultimately land on your website and find your products so that they can begin shopping with you. There are two different ways that you can drive people into your website: directly or indirectly.

Directly driving people to your website means that you make one post and it immediately sends people through to your website so that they can start shopping with your brand. You do this anytime you make a post that encourages people to go to the link in your bio and start shopping for the product or service that you were talking about in your post. You can also have the same impact by sending people to your link through your stories or through your IGTV channel. As long as you are directly asking someone to go to your link, you are directly channeling them through your funnel. This means that indirect funnels will have a direct element – since at some point you are going to need to bounce people from your Instagram profile to your website.

Indirect sales funnels are a great way to provide your audience with plenty of information before they leave your page to check out your website as you have directed them to. Since you are driving them through two or three posts, you can provide plenty of diverse insight and information on your product, service, or brand before they ultimately land on your website. There are many different ways that you can drive people around your Instagram profile, depending on what it is that you are trying to accomplish and what type of content you have to offer. For example, you can encourage someone watching your story to go check out your post, and then, when they check out the post, you can have a piece written that encourages them to check out your latest IGTV video and then that video can lead people to your website. You can also have one post that directs people to your website and then use your stories, IGTV, and live video feed to drive everyone over to that story first, where they read your content before then clicking over to your website.

How you choose to funnel people through your page and onto your website is up to you, though you should always be doing this or working toward building a funnel to ensure that you are directing people over to where they can actually pay for your products or services. That being said, refrain from making every single post, story, and video based on marketing or funneling people around because people will quickly catch on to what you are doing and they will stop following you. Some of your posts should be solely based on attracting new audience members to your profile through valuable content, interesting information, high-quality images, and relationship-building strategies like those outlined previously in this book.

Of course, if you are building a sales funnel on your Instagram profile, it is only natural that you include that sales funnel on your website too. When people land on your website, they should very clearly be drawn through your website to learn more about who you are and what you have to offer before landing on a page where they can look over your products or services. This way, they already know that they like your brand and that they want to work with you or shop with you before they even land on your sales page. You should also have an e-mail capture popup appear on your website so that you can start capturing people's emails and building an email newsletter into your funnel. Remember: some people will need to land on your website several times before they actually pay for your products or services. You are going to need to continually funnel people over to your website and make your offers known so that people can continually land on your website and then make the decision actually to go ahead and purchase from you. Believe it or not, the more people land on your website, the more connected they feel to you, so even if they do not buy right away, they will remember their previous visits to your website and will begin to feel encouraged to shop with you the more they land there.

Local Marketing Strategies

Most of the strategies that we have been using to achieve new prospect clients are fairly broad and work great if you are running a global or remote business where the location of your clients is not entirely important. However, if you are running a local business, you are going to want to approach your marketing slightly differently so that you can reach your target audience in your local area. The way that you target your local market is simple, though it will require some intention and practice on your behalf to make sure that you are reaching the people that you are meant to reach.

The first thing that you should be doing is looking up local hashtags, especially ones that are related specifically to your industry. For example, if you are a candle maker, you can use hashtags like "#newyorkcandles" or "#calgarycandles" which are unique to your local area. You can also start using hashtags that are specific to entrepreneurs or certain relevant hobbies in your local area so that when you take pictures, you can use these hashtags and connect with other people in your area who would also be interested in what you have to offer. By using local hashtags in this way, you can ensure that you are reaching people who are close to you and accessing the local market which will likely be more relevant to your target audience.

Another way that you can market to your local audience is in-person, using strategies to get the people you meet in person on your Instagram account. Since you are likely using other in-person outreach methods to connect with your local audience, you can use this as an opportunity to have people follow you on Instagram and then using Instagram to keep them up-to-date on your latest offers, sales, and new products or services. Many brands will do this by informing people about their Instagram by word of mouth, including their Instagram handle on their business cards, and by putting their Instagram handle somewhere in their physical shop so that people can find it and see it. A particularly unique way that people are marketing in-person is by offering a photo op in their store where people can take pictures. In the photo op, they will generally include their store name and a unique hashtag that people can use to tag the store and their unique hashtag in their photograph, which not only connects the local audience with the brand but also creates free marketing. Another similar practice that has been used in coffee shops and cafés is having the Instagram logo drawn on the coffee board with the company's handle written next to it and a live tracker of how many followers the company has. Every time someone new follows them, they increase the number on the board so that they can share their growth with their personal audience right there in the store.

Ideally, you should be using as many different strategies as you can to drive your online audience to your in-person store, and your in-person store to your online platforms. The more you can connect with people both online and offline, the more relevant you stay in their lives, and therefore, the more likely you are to gain sales through your Instagram marketing strategies.

Designing Display Ads

The last way that you can really drive up sales from Instagram is through using display ads, which can be featured either in newsfeeds or story feeds, depending on what type of ad you choose to pay for. You can use one or the other, or ideally, you can use both on your platform so that you are reaching as many people as you can based on their preferred method of consuming content on Instagram. Should you have followers that prefer to consume content both through their feeds and their stories, they will come across your ads twice as often, which means that they will be twice as likely to click through and see what you have to offer.

There are three different types of display ads that you can offer on Instagram – videos, static images, and carousel images. Carousel images will not work on Instagram story ads, so you will need to choose a different method of advertising if you are going to be advertising through Instagram stories. Each ad has its own unique benefits, though the theme is that the more you get your brand in front of your audience, the more likely they are to click through and check out your website or follow you. Additionally, your display ads will target more than just your existing audience, which means that you have an additional channel working for you to help you bring in new followers and customers through Instagram.

You can set up your Instagram advertisements by going to your Facebook account and opening up an ads management account.

Then, you can go ahead and tap "Create Ad" on the left side of the screen and follow the prompts provided to you. Facebook's ads manager will ask you what your goals are with your advertisement, what you want the people who see your ad to do, and how you want to design the ad. You can then design it and choose which platforms you want it to run on, how, for how long, and with what budget. You will also determine whom you want to see the ad based on their demographics, interests, and whether or not they are already following you. Once you have set in these parameters, all you have to do is publish the ad, and it will begin showing up on all of the areas where you said it would.

When it comes to displaying ads, it is important that you use high-quality images that are very clear in what they are advertising so that your audience immediately knows what you are sharing with them and whether or not it engages their interest. You also need to use a caption that is direct, engaging, and interesting. Essentially, you should follow the exact steps outlined in Chapter 8. Make sure that you really give these posts your all so that you are creating something worthy of people stopping and paying attention to what it is that you are advertising for them.

If you are not tech savvy or you find yourself struggling to make effective images for advertisements, you might consider hiring a professional social media advertising agency to support you in creating high-quality advertisements. Many individuals are in the business of creating advertisements and putting them to work on social media so that you can start seeing better results from your paid ads. While this will cost you more money, since you are paying someone else to design your ads, they will also be more likely to gain traction, making them worth your investment.

Chapter 12: When Gurus Lie

Since the launch of Instagram, there have been many "gurus" coming out of the woodwork claiming that they know exactly how to get your posts viewed, grow your page faster, and get you seen. They claim to have the one-size-fits-all strategies should your page not be gaining traction, and that they can get you thousands of "real" followers overnight. Realistically, these gurus are typically spewing nonsense that will not actually support you in growing your page properly. In this chapter, we are going to talk about six very common myths that so-called marketing gurus and Instagram gurus talk about, and also tell you the truth.

Myth #1: Instagram Does Not Matter

The first myth commonly told by marketing gurus is that Instagram does not matter and that you can easily grow your business anywhere else without the use of Instagram. The reality is that Instagram is actually one of the largest social media platforms out there and virtually every single company can increase their audience and conversion ratio through Instagram if they use it properly. There are no specific models that work best on Instagram, as every company can get on Instagram and start creating a unique strategy that works best for them. If you have a company in the 21st century, you need to be building your audience on Instagram. Even if your audience consists primarily of seniors or children or people who would likely not be on Instagram, the people who will be supporting these individuals in purchasing things *will* be on Instagram.

Myth #2: You Can Get Shadow Banned

In 2018, a massive myth came around that you can get "shadow banned" on Instagram, which essentially means that Instagram will not show your posts to anyone on the platform. The truth is: shadow bans are not real. If you were going to get banned or have your images not seen by people on the platform, it would be a real ban, not a sneaky shadow ban that Instagram would not even bother to inform you about. What is typically happening when people claim to be shadowbanned is that they are not using effective marketing strategies, so they are not being seen by anyone else on the platform. The reality for why you are only getting minimal engagement is likely that you are not using effective posting and marketing strategies; therefore, your organic visibility is low, and you need to do more to get your visibility up. Consider using the strategies outlined earlier in this book to help you maximize your visibility and start gaining more followers on Instagram.

Myth #3: Video Content Does Not Matter

Many people feel intimidated by the creation of video content, and unfortunately, are being told by mediocre marketing strategists that they can effectively use the platform without video marketing. The truth is: you can use the platform and create success without videos, but you are not going to create nearly as much as you could if you were to incorporate video content into your strategy. At the end of the day, your followers want to feel connected with your brand and with the people who are running the brand, which is done best by creating video content for your followers to engage with. You can create video content through your stories, live videos, IGTV, or even creating short videos to use as posts or as display ads.

When you are creating videos, make sure that you create high-quality videos and that you focus on getting yourself comfortable on camera. Since video marketing is growing in popularity, many people are using high-quality equipment, professional lighting, and who are great on camera. While you do not need to have professional equipment or be a daytime television star, using a high-quality light or sitting in natural light, using a camera that shoots in at least 1080p (most new smartphones shoot in 1080p or 4k), and practicing frequently is crucial. The more you practice shooting videos, the more you are going to feel confident in creating them, and the better your videos are going to get over time. As you grow larger, you can also consider having a professional videographer working together with you to create professional videos for your advertisements and posts. Again, this is not necessary, but you can certainly do it if you want to step up your game and have higher quality content.

Myth #4: Engagement Just Happens

Another myth that is common in the marketing industry is saying that engagement just happens. This is in alignment with "create it, and they will come" – which is completely untrue. This myth was not accurate before the days of the internet, and it continues to remain inaccurate even with the internet in place. The basic truth is: it is not your followers' job to find you; it is your job to find them. You are the one creating products and services and seeking to get people to purchase them, so you need to be putting in the effort to get your brand in front of people and earning their trust and loyalty.

When you get on Instagram, make sure that you are ready to do what it takes to begin building engagement on the platform. As well, make sure that you are taking responsibility if you find that your engagement is not growing and you are not getting the number of followers that you desire to get. At the end of the day, the problem is not your followers but your inability to reach them effectively, so you will need to do what it takes to adjust your approach to get in front of your followers and get seen. If you find that you are not getting the results you desire, analyze your analytics and look for opportunities to begin creating a better impact on the platform.

Myth #5: Analytics Don't Matter

While you do not exactly have to pay attention to your analytics, you can almost guarantee that you are not going to generate the impact that you desire to have if you are not paying attention to your analytics on Instagram. Your analytics literally tell you precisely what your audience likes, what they don't like, and what they want to see more of from you on your Instagram page. If you are not following your analytics and offering more content base on what your audience likes, you may be losing out on money because you are directly ignoring what your audience is telling you. When you are creating new content, always look at your analytics to see what your followers like the most and seek to create more content of that nature. If you are posting content that does not typically get many likes on your profile, see if you can borrow strategies from your more successful posts to create a higher quality post that earns better engagement. There are always ways that your analytics can support you in creating higher quality content, so do not overlook this information based on the false belief that "analytics do no matter".

Myth #6: Success is Guaranteed

Finally, as with anything, success is never guaranteed. The myth that you can get on Instagram and generate easy overnight success as a business owner is false, and in many cases, will become a dangerous waste of your time in business if you believe it. The strategy that you go into Instagram with may not be strong enough to carry your company to success on Instagram, and if you refuse to adapt to the platform and learn as you go, there may never come a day where you will experience success on the platform. Unfortunately, many people will tell you that you can guarantee your success if you follow certain strategies, behave a certain way, or participate in certain ways. The reality is: not everyone will generate success on Instagram because not everyone is prepared to undergo the learning curve of the platform and start working with it rather than in their own way. While authenticity and individuality are key, if you are not sharing stuff that people want to see and pay attention to, you simply will not gain traction on the platform. At the end of the day, Instagram is not for everyone, and if you are not prepared to endure the learning curve, learn how to read your analytics, create high-quality content, and grow with the platform, your success is not, in fact, going to be guaranteed.

Conclusion

Congratulations on completing the book *Instagram Marketing: How to Dominate Your Niche in 2019 with Your Small Business and Personal Brand by Marketing on a Super Popular Social Media Platform and Leveraging Its Influencers.*

This book was written to support you in launching or growing your business on Instagram in 2019. While it can be challenging to determine exactly what new features will come out in 2019 or what trends will rise, one thing is for sure – some trends are not going anywhere and will likely evolve over the course of 2019. If you want to grow your business massively on this platform, you need to do your best to stay on board with these changes, put in the work to establish yourself, and focus on creating consistency in your Instagram approach. The more consistent you remain, the larger your following will grow and the more retained followers you will have due to your consistent branding and engagement.

I hope that through reading this book, you are now feeling more confident in establishing a powerful Instagram marketing strategy that you can use to approach Instagram in 2019. From generating high-quality content to getting that content in front of your audience and learning how to increase your engagement, there are many strategies required in growing your Instagram account. That being said, once you learn how the process works, using Instagram will seem effortless, and your growth will continue to maximize over time. The initial learning stages are the most challenging, but once you hit your stride, it becomes much easier to grow on Instagram or any other platform that you may use to grow your business online.

Remember: as you build your account, always seek to create sales funnels that you can use to drive people from your profile to your website so that they can begin learning about your products and services. Although they may not purchase from you the first time they land on your page, the more they find themselves landing on your website, the more likely they will be to purchase something from your company. Plus, this is a great way to get new followers over to your website so that you can start building recognition and interest with new followers as well.

After you have completed reading this book, your best course of action is to ensure that your account is branded, start creating an attractive image on your account, and then start building your following using the strategies proposed in this very book! Once you have laid out the foundation, you simply need to remain consistent to create your growth.

Lastly, if you enjoyed the book, and felt that it supported you in understanding how you can best approach Instagram in 2019, please take the time honestly to review it on Amazon Kindle.

Thank you and best of luck in 2019!

Description

Instagram is one of the largest social media platforms in the world, and the platform is rapidly growing into one of the most powerful online marketing tools for small businesses and personal brands. If you are currently in business, or if you are planning on launching a business in 2019, you need to get your business on Instagram and start building engagement on this social media giant.

As Instagram continues to expand, it creates more unique opportunities for brands to engage with their audience, develop an interactive relationship with their prospects, and start funneling people over to their websites. Most recently, Instagram has included stories, live video, and IGTV features on its platform to facilitate for this connection. It is projected that 2019 will come with equally great opportunities and evolutions for brands to begin going even further in the process of creating powerful relationships with their audience.

If you are ready to start making an impact on Instagram in 2019, *Instagram Marketing: How to Dominate Your Niche in 2019 with Your Small Business and Personal Brand by Marketing on a Super Popular Social Media Platform and Leveraging Its Influencers* is the exact book you are looking for! In this book, you will learn about:

- Choosing your niche
- How to set up your Instagram profile
- Strategies for branding your account and all of the content that you post
- How to create powerful, scroll-stopping posts
- Making sales on Instagram
- Building Instagram into your sales funnel
- Myths from marketing gurus and the truth you need to know
- Five unwritten rules on Instagram
- And more!

If you are ready to master Instagram marketing in 2019, pick up your copy of *Instagram Marketing: How to Dominate Your Niche in 2019 with Your Small Business and Personal Brand by Marketing on a Super Popular Social Media Platform and Leveraging Its Influencers* today! By putting the strategies in this book to work, you will quickly find yourself rising to the top of the Instagram ladder and creating a massive impact between your brand and your audience.

Check out another book by Matt Golden

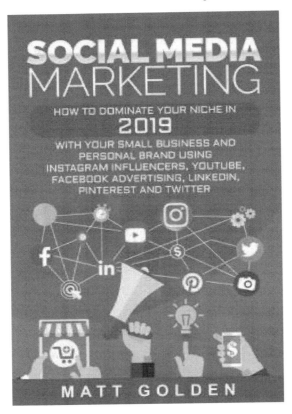

Printed in Poland
by Amazon Fulfillment
Poland Sp. z o.o., Wrocław